CREDIT STACKING

How to Access and Leverage Credit
to Start Businesses, Scale Your Business,
Or Fund Investments to Build a Life of Freedom

JACK MCCOLL

CREDIT STACKING
© 2022 by JACK MCCOLL

All rights reserved solely by the author. The author guarantees all contents are original and do not infringe upon the legal rights of any other person or work. No part of this book may be reproduced in any form without the permission of the author. The views expressed in this book are not necessarily those of the publisher.

Printed in the United States of America.
ISBN-13:
979-8-218-00141-4 Paperback
979-8-218-00142-1 Hardcover

Library of Congress Control Number: 2022909341

McColl Publishing
Seattle, WA

Typeset by: Michelle Cline

FOREWORD

If you're reading this book, it means you have an idea or business that you are trying to launch and simply need the necessary resources to create momentum. If you've been here before, like I have, you know that the only thing keeping your dream on the ground is a lack of resources. Whether that resource is time, property, materials, or tools, its absence can leave a million-dollar business as nothing more than an idea scribbled in a notebook. In this book, I want to show you something that I wish someone had shown me when I began my journey at twenty. All the resources needed to build any business have something in common. Whether you're building a real estate business, marketing business, e-commerce, brick-and-mortar gift store, coffee shop, or financial wellness program, your resources will all have one thing in common: they all need capital to obtain. Capital is the common feature of every tool in your toolbox and is, without a doubt, the feature most sought after by the everyday entrepreneur. Even Richard Branson, the founder of Virgin Group and, is known for saying that "your primary job as an entrepreneur," is to raise capital. He goes as far as to say, "by any means necessary," meaning from banks, family, or investors. You and I know him today as a man known for taking big risks and founding a record label from a small shop. But without this mentality of raising capital, his record business and future ventures in an airline, hotel line, and mobile-phone carrier would have died in that one building in London. Having now been in the business of entrepreneurship for eight years, I can promise you, this is no exaggeration. Your ideas are funded, or they die. In fact, my work life has been just as involved in raising capital as it has been involved in utilizing that capital to generate income. If you're finding yourself in that same small shop, or if you haven't even built the shop yet, then I absolutely encourage you to keep reading. I will take you through a method of raising capital that has helped me create value and profit while enjoying travel, freedom, and peace of mind. My method of credit stacking helps you navigate the business credit card market with the goal of obtaining a line of credit that can help you launch your business, expand your inventory, or simply obtain the life on the road that you have always wanted.

Through credit stacking, you can obtain adequate capital to make these dreams a reality with minimal risk to yourself or your personal finances. I'm going to walk through the same exact strategies that I have used to go from zero business credit cards to getting approved for ~$500,000 in approved credit in just fourteen months. The same strategies that are also helping hundreds of entrepreneurs get access to over $100K of 0-percent interest business credit in as little as thirty days of implementing them. There isn't a single entrepreneur (whether they have a business already or not) these strategies won't help to get access to large amounts of 0-percent capital and accelerate them to financial freedom.

Now, I know what you're probably thinking, "Jack, that sounds too risky," and were you just applying for a bunch of credit cards online and spending wildly with them, I'd 100 percent agree with you. You might be thinking it won't work for you because you have bad credit, bad experiences with credit cards, or just don't like the idea of leveraging your projects with debt. I'll level with you; this method is not the standard path to funding and isn't something you'll ever take a course on in business school. This book contains hacks and guides to steer you clear of unnecessary risk, fees, and credit card rejection.

Foreword

Knowing that you may still have reservations, I want to ask you to approach this method with an open mind. This method can work with any traditional funding model you are currently following or can be your sole funding strategy. Either way, it will break a few rules that you may think exist in the credit card industry. The traditional approaches that operate within these rules may give you a good, solid source of funding but will not be able to accelerate your capital growth and expansion like credit stacking can. To quote my hero, John D. Rockefeller, "Don't be afraid to give up the good to go for the great." Leave everything you think you know about credit cards, borrowing, or funding at the door, and give me the chance to show you just how much credit stacking can do for you.

The most important thing for a young man is to establish credit—A reputation and character. — John D Rockefeller

TABLE OF CONTENTS

Foreword iii

Introduction   My Story ix

Chapter 1   Where Do You Want to Go? 1

Chapter 2   Personal Credit 11

Chapter 3   Credit Cards and Calculated Risk 31

Chapter 4   Using Business Credit to Gain Momentum 51

Chapter 5   Money 89

Chapter 6   Traveling on Credit 117

Chapter 7   The Road to Independence 151

Glossary 159

INTRODUCTION
MY STORY

I mentioned before that I wish I had discovered the steps in this book earlier in life, and that was no exaggeration. If I could go back and teach myself at twenty the knowledge that I have now about how to credit stack to fund my businesses, I could have begun my journey with less risk, more momentum, and peace of mind. Those early years of mine as an entrepreneur were years with just as many successes as failures. I learned so much from trial and error and would not trade those lessons for anything. As my mindset has always been to learn from mistakes, I don't see those years as wasted or squandered. They gave me the drive to find methods that work and to put my experiences to work for both myself and others on the same path. Even with all that growth I was able to experience, there was room for my ventures to be optimized. Looking back now, eight years later, I can see so many opportunities a program like this could have opened my eyes to. It is my goal to use this mindset in coaching you through whatever stage of entrepreneurship you may be in. If you're just starting out, this plan can help accelerate you to your first profits. If your business is well established but you want to expand, this plan can help you achieve higher sales numbers. If you've worked your way to a place of financial independence and want to travel full time, this plan can give you the tools to achieve that goal. Whatever your vision is, with an effective plan to raise capital, you can make it a reality.

The first dreams I saw someone make into a reality were my dad's. When I talk about my goals for my business, or my goals for your business, it is impossible to not think back on all the lessons he taught me as a boy and later as a young business owner. My dad has been the owner of a software business for as long as I can remember. As a business owner and a father, he made it his goal to maintain a successful business but not at the expense of his family. His successful utilization of his own financial freedom gave him the time and resources to spend more time with his family. He built his own freedom and time. Watching this had a lasting impact on my brother and me. I would go so far as to say that without the example of my father to guide and teach me in my early years, I would have probably not had as much direction or drive to be effective in my endeavors.

Part of his influence on me was in his encouraging me to pursue a dual credit program as a high schooler. I'm sure you are familiar with these kinds of programs. They give you the opportunity to take college credit while still in high school. In the long run, this helps you save time and money in college. You can finish your degree earlier, pursue a career earlier, and, overall, save money, time, and energy. It certainly was a boost for me. It was just that little bit of acceleration that I needed to move forward with my dreams at a younger age. That was just how my dad thought. Why waste time and money on something when it won't bring you happiness or fulfillment in the end? Why waste time and energy when you could be using those finite resources to grind toward your goals? After following his advice with that program, I was able to gain experience as a videographer and had a good, successful snowboarding career, gaining sponsorship deals and offers for my work in videography. I feel like I would have remained a successful snowboarder, but I sustained a pretty bad injury on the slopes that prematurely ended my career. At the time, I really didn't know what to do. I had no jobs lined up, no snowboarding career with sponsorship deals, and no clear direction. The only thing I knew is that I needed to find something else to do. But, as you'll find happens so often in business, your lows can be followed by periods of aggressive acceleration and growth.

I was soon contacted with an offer from the app Yik Yak to help them promote their app on college campuses. After having the opportunity to work with the amazing team at Yik Yak, I was able to then pursue several ventures from selling inflatable loungers to hover boards, a travel company with my brother, and an Airbnb venture in Bali. The lessons that I learned during this time still stick with me as I continue in business today. In fact, the first time I ever checked my credit score was about the same time I learned about business credit. I've been pretty active on personal credit cards. I saw the ones with the best travel rewards and sign-up bonuses. I would always paid on time, but I didn't understand the power of credit. While I was in Bali, Indonesia, I met someone through a mutual friend. We were sitting at a café, and he was applying for several business credit cards. We discussed business cards for the better part of an hour, and I quickly realized that I needed to be using this. I jumped in with both feet. Over the next few months, I was contacting successful entrepreneurs I knew, joining paid Facebook groups, high-level mentorship programs, and learning about business credit from anyone that seemed like a credible source.

Eventually, we had to close our Airbnbs in Bali because of Covid-19. That gave me plenty of time to jump into this credit world I was studying. Soon, I was offering my advice to others for free. I used this period as sort of a test of what I knew. When I saw others were experiencing similar results in gaining access to capital through credit, I knew I was on to something. Probably the biggest thing to my growth in understanding credit were these free consultations as well as the relationships I built with relationship managers at the banks. I was calling them so often and learning to ask the right questions to get the information I needed. After four months of this intense immersion in the world of credit, my next step was clear. It was time to scale what

I was doing. It started as free strategy sessions with people, then I started a website and started selling courses and hosting classes. For the last couple of years, I have spent my time helping aspiring and seasoned entrepreneurs to gain access to capital and scale their businesses through a method called credit stacking.

I'm telling you all of this to show you that I have been through the highs and lows of business. It's an understatement to say it can be hard; it can be completely crushing and feel impossible at times. I've been able to progress through all these steps with several different businesses. This progression has taught me new lessons with each step that I want to share with you here. While the focus of this book and my online course is to teach you about the advantages of credit stacking, the lessons I've learned along the way will be included to help you steer clear of mistakes that are often made and to pursue processes and systems that result in high returns. I'll be with you through each step to mentor and support you as you maximize your potential.

With the right mindset, vision, and drive, we can accomplish anything. So, let's waste no time and dig right into the steps that you can take to accelerate achievements and maximize your returns.

Thank you for making the time to dive into Credit Stacking, I'm excited for the things you will learn throughout this book! If you find yourself loving it and want to share it with others, please feel free to post a picture of the book on your Instagram story so others can grab it as well! Also, if you tag me (@kingofdebt) I will repost your IG Story of it. Thanks so much, and I wish you the best!

Jack McColl

CHAPTER 1
WHERE DO YOU WANT TO GO?

The first step towards getting somewhere is to decide you're not going to stay where you are.

J. P. Morgan

What does success look like to you? Depending on your values and pursuits, the answer to this question will look very different. If you're a business owner, it may look like a successfully-launched business plan. If you're a travel blogger, journalist, or social media influencer, it may look like the ability to fund trips to locations that will provide you with content and experience. For some, success looks like time and travel. For others, it looks like freedom and flexibility. Going back to my dad, his goals were making time for his family while also running his software business. While it may seem like a small point, it is crucial to develop your definition of success before you ever attempt to attain it. Defining your definition of success and how you will reach that kind of success is your vision. Through this vision, you will be able to set your goals to make this vision a reality. Before we start this journey, I want you to stop and visualize those goals. Consider the steps it will take to make your vision your reality. The reason it is so important to make this your first step is that no funding plan, business plan, or amount of hard work can ever compensate for a lack of vision. The steps we are going to go over and the techniques and hacks I'll share with you will never correct poor vision. Before we move on, go ahead and take some time. Develop those goals, define that vision, and journal it. Journaling is going to make all the difference in your process. Once you have that vision on paper, you're going to be able to understand it much better than you did just thinking about it. To help you with this process, I have a couple of tools that I like to give out in my coaching. These same questions can be found in my online course and can help you write out your idea of a dream life:

- Where do you want to live?
- What relationship do you want to have?
- What career do you want?
- How much do you want to make?
- What do you want to be invested in?
- What do you want to do for fun?

After you write down these questions, take a break from reading, journal your vision, and meet me in the next paragraph.

How do your goals seem to you now? Do you feel that your vision is clearly defined? If you have a clear goal written down in front of you, then we'll move on to your steps to success. If you don't, then I would strongly advise going back and reconsidering your goals and vision before you move on. I cannot emphasize enough how important this step is. You can have all the energy and drive necessary to push your vision forward, but without direction and a clear goal, you will end up exhausted and frustrated. As time goes on, you'll find this can be helped by journaling your thoughts. I make it a habit to journal at least once a day. When I do so, I try to add things that I am grateful for, affirmations for myself, a recent win, desires, and a power list of needle-moving things that are accomplishable today. This strategy has helped me reach goals and maintain momentum along the way. While you're on this journey, adopting a journaling habit and being disciplined to stay with it can help you keep track of your growth and keep yourself accountable to meet your goals on a regular basis.

Now that you have a method to track your progress, the next step is to check in on your discipline, resilience, and environment. Going forward, you're going to need discipline to maintain your productivity. After a while in this pattern of discipline, you're then going to realize that you need resilience. And if you're like many self-starters, you're going to find you're only as good as your environment. If you haven't created a productive environment, you won't reach your full potential. Before we dive into the technical aspects of raising capital, you need to stop here and have an honest conversation with yourself about what it is you need to do to make these business strategies work. The purpose of this portion is to keep yourself free from decisions that may be too emotional or illogical. We'll address the discipline and resilience at the same time, as they tend to work off each other. Then we'll go over how your environment can give you the cutting edge that you need to create and grow unimpeded by negative people, environments, or habits. Understanding how to gain discipline and resilience, as well as how to control and design your environment, will be the deciding factor in your path to success.

MAINTAIN DISCIPLINE

The alarm goes off. You immediately jam that "snooze" option on your phone screen because you don't feel like waking up to the challenges that day. You know you're launching your business, you know you only have twenty-four hours in a day, and you know that you can't experience growth just lying there in bed. What's happened here is an emotional decision was made instead of one using logic and discipline. It might be tempting to call it a one-time incident and think it won't become a regular thing. But that thinking is exactly what you are going to need to separate yourself from if you want this program to work for you. There's a man whose advice I've found to be immeasurably valuable named Grant Cardone. I'm sure you've heard about his story of rags to riches, using debt to purchase his massive real estate fortune and earning his first million before thirty. His influence has been significant in my life and career, and I highly recommend you follow his social media and videos, as they are a treasure trove of knowledge and motivation. Grant stated once that to be successful in business, you must, "Do the things you don't wanna do, so that one day you can do the things that you wanna do. Pay the price! Sacrifice something!" What he's talking about is the discipline to get yourself out of bed and go. There might be techniques and tricks to help with that in the same way we're going over techniques and tricks for funding in this book. But in the end, it will all boil down to the discipline to maintain those tricks and hacks. It's all about the disciplines that you commit to every day.

Are you making those meetings?

Are you making those cold calls?

Are you doing those pushups or pullups you swore you'd be doing in your New Year's resolution?

These are the kinds of things that are going to make the difference in the long run. As a point of experience, my brother and I organized a travel business for young people visiting Cabo back in my early twenties. I wouldn't trade those days for anything, but there were some tough trials along the way. We had to deal with a particular travel restriction (Covid-19) that almost crippled the business. During those days, the potential for losing business meant that we had to put in twice the hours and at least twice the effort to keep the business going. Our normal target customer wasn't going to meet our revenue needs, meaning we had to go pound the pavement and make those revenue needs with customers that we would not have normally had to rely on. This took discipline to see through and was not easy in the slightest. Think about that when you're tempted to just sit back and think sales will come to you, or that cold calls will just get your voicemail and call you back. Those mornings where you make a promise to yourself that tomorrow you'll change, tomorrow you'll do differently, those are the days that will make or break your future success. You must maintain discipline. I say maintain because in a strange way, remaining disciplined is in and of itself a form of discipline. You will need discipline to keep you on track and discipline to drive you to the next level. Each day when you wake up, it is highly likely that you will need to remind yourself of the disciplines you committed to the day before. But this is just part of the process and is a day-after-day repetition of the same principles. Some of these principles are that there are no excuses, no giving up, and no turning back. Only discipline.

DEVELOP RESILIENCE

Your key next step in the process is to develop your resilience. Resilience, in this case, can be defined as your ability to weather failure. We all fail. We all make mistakes, and we all fall on our face many times. It's simply a fact that on this path that you've chosen to take, you're going to fail over and over. It's important to cultivate resilience early in the process before you burn out or exhaust yourself. The point of training yourself for failure, as well as for success, is so you'll learn to see your failures as their own unique lessons for the future. I look back on mine, and I see lessons learned and experiences had. I've mentioned that the techniques I am teaching through this book were not something I understood early in my career. I've had several times where my ideas seemed to not be the long-term businesses that I had hoped they would be. Could I spend unnecessary time and energy banging my head against the wall at those failures? Well, sure. But I could also learn and grow from those experiences. I could see them for the great lessons that they have been and be thankful for the role they played in pushing me toward success. This is resilience, and it is something that you will see in the life of every successful entrepreneur. Couple this with the right mindset and discipline to rise and grind, and you'll find yourself achieving your dreams every single day.

MINDSET/ENVIRONMENT

The last two keys to your success in this course and business are your environment and mindset. These two often go hand in hand, and one can easily influence the other. The first of these two, mindset, can be broken down into two different kinds of mindsets. It's important to identify which kind you are right now or have been in the past. The two kinds of mindsets in people can be categorized as a growth mindset and a fixed mindset. Each person on earth is of one mindset or the other. To explain what this means, if you're of a fixed mindset, you probably view mistakes as unavoidable fate, feel that your failures limit you, and stick to the things you know. As the name implies, you don't live up to your potential but hold yourself back to feel comfortable with where you are. This is a limiting mindset, as we'll discuss in a minute. The other mindset, the growth mindset, is where you see your mistakes as corrections to be made for next time, your failures as opportunities for growth, and the things that you don't know as concepts and knowledge that you want to attain. You see those concepts as things that can make you a better version of yourself. I don't think I have to tell you which way to live. If one is called a growth mindset, the other is most definitely anti-growth. There is no doubt in my mind that you can change your mindset from one that is limiting you to one that is helping you grow. That change is going to be essential going forward. In fact, just go ahead and state it to yourself: "I'm (insert your name here), and I can do anything!" This is an excellent piece of affirmation to add to your journaling that you've hopefully begun for this book. You need to find what areas of your mindset are holding you back and work them out of your system. In working through these mindsets, you'll find yourself in a much better place for growth.

Once you've worked through those limiting mindsets, the next thing to really scrutinize and design for your success is your environment. I am a firm believer that each of us is a product of our environment. Whether it's entrepreneurship, fitness, or education, you cannot deny the fact that the environment you put yourself in is going to greatly influence your success in that field or activity. This is why students go to libraries to study, many fitness enthusiasts find a gym helps them focus on their workout, and many entrepreneurs, like me, find motivational groups of people and work environments to be the best for networking, growth, and building the life you want. If you think you can be productive in an environment that does not foster productivity, then you're simply pushing up a hill at a steeper grade than you have to. And honestly, why would you want to do that? There's no purpose in unnecessarily stressing yourself out in a location or situation that won't produce optimal efficiency.

No joke, I have gone and rented a hotel room just to get away from distractions for prolonged periods of time when I've had work and projects I absolutely had to focus on. Whatever the method is to alter your environment, you need to be ready to take that step and put yourself in a better position to concentrate, grind out the projects in your way, and not get distracted by the world around you.

It is simply too difficult to focus in some environments and grow in others. The good news is that this is absolutely something that you can change. For example, if you're trying to get through this book in a certain amount of time, and you need to cancel a subscription to a streaming service to do it, that is changing your environment. If you have found a room in your home or a spot where you can just grind out the work without distractions, claiming that space and working your hardest there is changing your environment. These are all steps that you can take. One part of this process that I've found is actually very difficult for many is in the part of dealing with people. If you find yourself surrounded by people who are limiting your potential or who may just not have any similar goals as yours, then you may be doing yourself a favor by limiting the amount of time you spend around those people. It's not that you must cut people completely out of your life, but rather a controlled limitation on how much influence you allow them to have on your time and productivity. Being disciplined to keep your environment controlled can be a very difficult part of the process. Many writers have even moved to different states, cities, or countries because they found it was more conducive to their creative process. And if moving is necessary to network with the people you want to grow around and learn from, then you are doing yourself a disservice by not making that big move.

To summarize, you must always maintain your discipline but especially during the hard times. Your discipline will pay off if you stay resilient and work to cultivate a mindset of growth and an environment that fuels your success. With these principles established, you will be in the right place and frame of mind to apply these credit stacking techniques.

Before we get into the credit stacking strategies, there are a few technical aspects of the business that it would be best to learn now. The world of business credit has so many hidden fees, features, and criteria that it is impossible to navigate without some understanding of how the process works. In the glossary on page (insert page number), you'll find a list of terms that are essential to memorize and understand. We'll discuss these in greater detail throughout the book. It would be a good idea to go ahead and familiarize yourself with them right now from the glossary in the back of the book.

GOOD DEBT VS. BAD DEBT

Debt is something that can ruin someone or make them the best version of themselves financially. It's truly a tool that can be used for the greater or worse, and at the end of the day, it comes down to how it's used. When classifying debt, I want to be clear about the two categories of debt. There is good debt, and there is bad debt, and each kind is very clear based on one thing: is the debt an asset to your financial growth, or is it a liability? Is it helping you make more money, or is it only costing you money? One way to determine that is by asking yourself if the debt is invested into assets that are appreciating or assisting you with increasing cash flow or invested into liabilities that are depreciating or reducing cash flow. For example, debt invested into a business or something like an investment property would be classified as "good debt" since this debt helps you increase your cash flow or buy an asset that is appreciating in value, essentially putting yourself in a better financial position. In contrast, if the debt was used to fund a vacation, medical procedure, or a car for personal use, this would be an example of bad debt since these purchases won't necessarily help you increase cash flow or appreciate in value. These types of transactions might be important and necessary for you, but they don't provide a direct correlation in improving your financial position. After I was able to access ~$500K in credit, I was very strict on only allocating it to things that assisted me in increasing my cash flow or increasing the value of my net worth. For anything else, I would allocate my active or passive income to cover these expenses. Debt is a tool at your discretion, so please, before allocating money, ask yourself what kind of investment or purchase it is to best enable yourself on smart financial decisions.

CHAPTER 2
PERSONAL CREDIT

"Concentrate your energy, your thoughts and your capital."

Andrew Carnegie

PERSONAL CREDIT

Before we dive into the specific benefits that credit provides, I really want to paint the picture on how crucial your personal credit is for getting access to capital and accelerating financial freedom. Not only will your personal credit profile help you get elite personal credit cards, which can save you tens of thousands of dollars through its perks and rewards (cash back and free travel), but a strong personal credit profile can save you hundreds of thousands of dollar through the low rates on auto loans and mortgages you will be getting approved for in your lifetime. Additionally, good credit will assist with getting approved for renting an apartment, financing things like cell phones, and getting discounts on insurance. It's truly a staple of getting ahead in life.

Now that we have the basics covered on the importance of good credit, I want to explain to you why it's REALLY important to have good credit, specifically if you are an entrepreneur, aspiring entrepreneur, or investor. When it comes to getting approved for business credit, your personal credit is the foundation and a crucial element in getting approved for $50K+ 0-percent interest business credit cards. Business credit is something we are going to cover in thorough detail in the next chapter, but I want to emphasize how crucial your personal credit profile is in leading you to accessing hundreds of thousands of 0-percent interest capital that you can use to start a business, scale a business, or make investments with. Simply put, the stronger your personal credit is, the more 0-percent interest capital you will get access to (even on brand new businesses!). So please take notes through this chapter and get excited for the Business Credit chapter because that is where we really accelerate.

AWARENESS

Now that you've covered the basic discipline and mindset required to succeed, we'll begin to dive into the nuts and bolts of credit stacking. This technique is something that, while technical and difficult-looking at first, is actually very simple and easy to navigate once you get familiar with the terminology and credit approval processes. By the end, you'll be an expert at analyzing business credit cards and getting approved for amazing perks and capital sources.

Before we start discussing the actual numerical factors to business credit, I want to make sure you understand how to carry out a credit analysis. *Awareness* is always the first step in anything. Just like a football calling a play or an entrepreneur making an investment, the crucial first step is awareness so you can understand exactly where you are in the game to make your best judgment on the next move. Without awareness, any plan you make will often lead to failure for most.

In this section, we'll be analyzing your credit score from different bureaus to best understand where you are at in the eyes of the bureaus or banks who will be looking at your credit profile. While this may sound like you need to do the actual number-crunching of a credit rating agency like Experian, I can promise you it's much simpler than that.

There are three credit bureaus where you'll be checking your credit score, which are the same three agencies that the banks will be checking when you submit a credit card application: Experian (EX), Equifax (EQ), and Transunion (TU). You can go online and check your score through these agencies or through apps that will show you a comparison of the three bureaus. You'll find that the different bureaus will rate you differently, based on what is reporting to each. Since banks or lenders can report differently to each bureau, and each bank can check a different bureau, it's crucial to make sure you are checking all three while analyzing your credit profile. In Credit Stacking, we actually have a specific template we ask our students to complete that helps break down the different credit factors so I can personally help them make the most strategic and effective plan moving forward.

When checking your credit, there are a variety of ways you can do this, some ways being free and some that require a payment. The next thing to understand is there are two different scoring systems in evaluating your risk to banks; there is your VantageScore and your FICO score. Both are rated out of 850 and ultimately indicate your level of risk to the lender; <500 being very risky and anything above 700 shows that you are low-risk when borrowing money. VantageScore is much more readily available and often free, but the banks will be checking (or "pulling") your FICO credit report. If the banks pull your FICO report, that is the report that we also want to be checking to ensure the highest level of success on approvals and limits. I personally use both scores to help me keep accurate awareness of my credit because even though VantageScore will often show a different score compared to FICO, it still helps me understand my utilization on each credit account (amount of debt that I'm using), number of hard inquiries, and things like average age or derogatory items. VantageScore is free to check on the Credit Karma app and updated more frequently, which makes it convenient to check, but the app only shows your reports for Equifax and Transunion (and doesn't show Experian). I recommend you download the Credit Karma app so you can check your credit.

However, before I submit ANY credit application, I will ANYWAYS check my FICO credit report since I know for a fact that the bank or lender will be looking at this report. For checking your FICO credit report, I personally use MyScoreIQ.com for three reasons:

1. Shows FICO score on a user friendly interface;
2. Provides up to one million dollars in identity theft protection in case your identity is stolen; and
3. Its interface connects to most credit repair companies' customer relationship management systems, which facilitates them in any services that they would need to do for you, such as remove any late payments, collections, hard inquiries, and so on. The most common is removing hard inquiries, which is something I do frequently as you will learn why in future chapters.

MyScoreIQ is a monthly subscription service that costs $35.99 per month for monthly FICO reports. As that may sound expensive to some, it's crucial to assist you in awareness of your credit profile as you proceed on your credit journey.
When checking your credit profile on the three bureaus, if it is discouraging or seems to be lower than what you're looking for, don't worry about it. No matter how low or weak your credit score is, the

beauty is it is always fixable! Even if you have collections, high utilization, or late payments, these are things you can reverse, which will help you reach a 700+ credit score. There is absolutely no reason why anyone reading this book should have under a 700 credit score. If that is you, please just know that it is only temporary, and with the right information and strategies, you will easily be able to join the 700 or even 800 club! Additionally, some people think that the more credit you get, the worse your score can be. Not there can be some sense in that is you are not maintaining your credit properly, but I am here to tell you it will actually increase your scores with the information outlined in this book. Even after getting approved for $500K in credit, I am able to maintain an 800+ FICO score. Here is a screenshot from MyScoreIQ report to show you:

This course has helped many obtain direct access to business credit in addition to the deeper understanding of the process. For now, creating that tool for yourself to assess your own credit score will be instrumental in understanding your ability to raise capital. While there are apps for this that compare the different scores, make sure you're careful of the promotions for high-interest loans that they offer there. They can be attractive but will handicap you in the long run with their high interest and lack of perks. Now that you have an idea of the analysis process, you'll know what you're up against or what you have going for you in the following steps.

FACTORS OF YOUR CREDIT SCORE

There are five major things that can affect your scores that make up different percentages of your total score:

1. Payment History – 35%
   - This one shows how well you've made your payments on time.
   - Payment history is the most important factor.
     - Harmed by
       - Paying late will greatly affect this portion and your total score as it will imply you cannot manage your payments well.
     - Helped by
       - Paying on time and keeping your cards from carrying balances
       - Having the autopay feature on
2. Amounts of Debt – 30%
   - Amount of collective limits
   - Sum of all the debt you are utilizing
   - 5–7% utilization is ideal
   - Length of Credit – 15%
   - A longer credit history will increase your score.
   - It's important to start establishing credit early to take advantage of this.
   - Can be supplemented by authorized users
3. Credit Mix – 10%
   - Having different kinds of credit products, not just cards, will increase your credit mix portion of your score.

- Having an auto loan, mortgage, or small installment loan will strengthen your credit mix
4. New Credit – 10%
    - This final category keeps track of how many new accounts you have opened or tried to open, primarily in the last six months.
    - The key here is hard inquiries. If there has been an inquiry made as you apply for new cards or lines of credit, then it will show up here and affect your score.

PAYMENT HISTORY

Since Payment History makes up 35 percent, it's the most significant section of your score and something worth prioritizing. This portion of your score consists of making payments on time; ideally you will want 99 percent+ on payment history. Additionally, you want to make sure that you maintain these cards you've opened. Keep using them on a regular basis. When it comes to the Grade A bank personal credit cards, such as at Chase, Amex, Bank of America, or US Bank, these are cards you want to use frequently for your normal spending, but for the cards at smaller banks where it doesn't make sense to build a relationship with such as any store cards, Discover, Apple Card, or card from small banks, instead of not using them completely, you will want to actually make at least one transaction on them each month to keep them active. This will show a strong payment history on your credit profile and also reduce the risk of the credit card account being shut down since banks will do this if a credit card is inactive for too long. Maybe it's just buying a pack of gum at a gas station one day or even setting up one to pay your monthly streaming subscription, applying autopay, and leaving it alone. This method will keep these accounts open and provide you with more on-time payments of balances, which will ultimately strengthen your credit score. Speaking of autopay, this is something that is crucial to making sure you NEVER miss a payment. Paying a bill less than thirty days late will not be reported to the credit bureaus, whereas a thirty+ day late will be reported. But even if the bank doesn't report your <30-day late payment, it still will have a negative effect on your approvals and limits with that specific bank, and this is why it's crucial you NEVER miss a payment EVER. There are also different levels of late payments that have different weights on your credit profile. There is a thirty-day late payment, a sixty-day late payment, and a ninety-day late payment, where each affects your credit score more severely. Please do me a favor and turn on your autopay feature for every single one of your credit card accounts, the risk vs. reward of not doing this just doesn't make sense. At minimum, set it to the minimum balance owed so you can avoid late payments, and then you can manually pay the amount of the balance you'd like at any given time. Please don't miss a payment. Trust me, it's just such a silly mistake that will set you back months, and that's the last thing I want to see for you. PS: Also please make sure that when your autopay feature is turned on or when you're making payments that there is actually enough money in the bank account that you're withdrawing from to make the payment. If not, you'll receive an insufficient fund flag, and that is very bad to keep a healthy relationship with that bank.

AMOUNT OF DEBT

In this factor of your credit profile, it's broken down into two parts; Total amount of debt that's lent to you and the amount of debt you are using (utilization).

First, we are going to focus on the total amount of debt that is being lent to you, and this is also referred to as "comparable credit" since when you eventually apply for business credit cards, the banks will be looking at your collective limits on the personal side. Business card limits are often larger, but that is usually only enabled by having decent limits on the personal side. If you only have $500–$2000 limits on personal cards, it's going to be very hard to get a $50K 0-percent interest card, at the moment at least before I help you increase the limits and in the next chapter show you how to get high limit personal cards.

If you have a good reputation with the banks you operate with, they are more than happy to loan you more money in the form of a credit line increase (CLI). What this means is that you go and apply for an increase in your credit line directly with the bank. Go ahead and do this six months after you've spent your first balances on those cards to ensure they'll work with you to get you the new credit limit that you need. Waiting this long is beneficial to the process of getting approved for an increase and waiting no longer than that is ideal for boosting your credit needs and available credit line. Whatever needs you have can be your reason for getting this increase, but it's important that you make sure you have a strategy behind your reason for the increase. The key is to have a reason and a solid strategy behind your financing plans; this can be anything from expanding a portion of your business to helping repair a vehicle to ensure you get your work done more efficiently or using the card to finance renovations in your house. They're likely not going to just expand it for no good reason. So give them a reason that makes sense and is a reasonable request. The cool thing about a CLI is that some banks will do this for you with only a soft credit check (doesn't affect your credit score). Any bank that doesn't pull your credit for a CLI is an absolute brainer to do. Additionally, some banks have hidden rules on how much you are able to increase the limit per request, where other banks are strictly based on your previous activity on the card. For the banks that do require a hard pull for a CLI, it's situational that I accept the additional inquiry depending on the specific bank, current limit, and my overall strategy.

Another step on optimizing your Amount of Debt section of your credit profile is to keep your reports showing under 10-percent utilization. And not just 10 percent on average across your credit report, but 10 percent on each and every revolving account is how you can produce the strongest score in this section of your FICO score.

How do you do this?

Won't the bureaus show your transactions, regardless? Well, no actually. Not if you pay off that card three to five days early. You can do this easily by setting up your auto pay early, checking on your balance, and paying off whatever may be left of the balance before three to five days of when your payment is due. Remember, this is the due date; note that date we've already discussed before that's thirty days after the actual due date. You pay it off early, and you won't have to worry about any issues with reports going to the credit bureaus. And also remember <10 percent is best, technically 5–7 percent is the sweet spot so banks can see you are actually using a little bit of the debt that is lent to you. Even if you max the card out in the month but pay it down before the due date, other banks, when they pull your credit, will only see what is reported to the credit bureaus.

One time, I had one of my personal credit card balances left at 95-percent utilization with a balance of about $20,000. Generally I will always float around the 800 FICO score mark, but when I floated this large of a balance over my statement closing date, my score dropped by almost 100 points! It's crazy how low your credit score can drop when you have high utilization. But, the good thing is I paid it off on the following statement, and my score shot up right back when it was before, just under 800.

LENGTH OF CREDIT

When it comes to the Length of Credit, this is a section that shows lenders how experienced you are with borrowing money in terms of amount of time in the game. Generally, someone who is older is wiser, and that is certainly how the banks see it on your credit profile.

If you have well-aged accounts with a strong average-aged credit profile, this will make you look less risky in the eyes of the banks. For this reason, it's very helpful to open accounts as soon as possible in your life and keep them open. One of the biggest mistakes I see people make is closing credit card accounts. It is certainly in your best interests to keep credit card accounts open, even if you don't use the card. I am a victim of this mistake as well. At one point, I had both the Chase Sapphire Preferred and Chase Sapphire Reserve, and because the Reserve's benefits are better across the board compared to the Preferred, I thought there was no reason for the Preferred, so I closed it. Rookie move, I must admit! But hey, I learned, and now I can share it with you. If the annual fee is the reason you want to close the account, a way to get around it is actually through a product change to avoid paying an annual fee that you prefer not to pay, but always keep your accounts open!

Maybe at this point, you have wondered, "Okay, I have a few credit card accounts, but what is considered well-aged?" Well, that is a great question, and it's really broken down into a few levels. At minimum, you are going to want to get your average age of your credit profile to above two years. If possible, you will want to see an average of five years of credit age, and, ideally, seven+ years. Each of those levels will have a significant impact on the Length of Credit factor of your credit score. Here is where it gets good, even if you don't have that much age at the moment on your accounts, you don't have to let your current credit account age many years to reach the ideal level I just mentioned. The secret sauce to get you a higher average age on your credit profile without actually aging them is taking advantage of something, Authorized Users (AUs). Essentially, what this allows you to do is piggyback off of the strength of someone else's credit card account. Most credit cards allow the card holder to add a variety of AUs onto the accounts, which is designed to give other people access to the same credit account, such as employees, spouses, or other family members. However, in this strategy, we are using it for a different purpose. Instead of actually giving the person who is added the physical credit card (which they can then use), the card holder has the ability to not provide the AU with the physical card, therefore the AU has zero access to the credit account. See, once a person is added as an AU, the credit account will now report on that person's credit report, not as a primary credit account but as an authorized user account. Authorized users' accounts are not weighted as heavily; however, it's a very easy way to add age to someone's credit report through this strategy. One thing that is incredibly important to note is that this strategy will only benefit you if you are being added as an AU to a strong account, and by strong, I mean has age that will increase your average age on your credit profile, consistently has low utilization, has no late payments, and has decent limits. If you get added to an account that doesn't check all four of those boxes, then it would most likely not benefit you. Low utilization and clean payment history on the account is crucial, but the next thing to look at is the age. AUs are most effective to add age to your credit profile, which can be very effective in increasing your credit score and allowing you to get approved for more elite cards with higher limits.

CASE STUDY

I would like to share a real-life example of this strategy at full effect. The story is about a twenty-three-year-old guy named Cooper, who is a recent college graduate. Naturally, since he is a bit younger and new to credit, the average age on his credit profile is very young. I've been working with Cooper now for the last six months, and in that time frame, I had him apply for a couple of specific strategic personal credit cards to build a stronger foundation but also instructed him to use the AU strategy to increase his average age. Once these AUs reported to his credit report, not only did it bump his score up from 695 to 745 (a fifty-point increase!), but it also dramatically increased his average. After this point, I gave him a few more pointers on optimizing his personal credit and building strategic bank relationships, which put him in a place where he was ready to go for his first business credit card. At this point, I made a personal introduction to my Business Relationship Manager at Chase Bank so we could submit his first business card application. I coached him on what information to input on the application, and soon after, I received a notification from him letting me know that we had approved for a $50K limit on his first business card ever! He was ecstatic! And I was too! Can you imagine being twenty-three and getting access to $50K of 0-percent interest capital? I certainly didn't have or have access to that kind of money just after graduating college. Cooper has both an e-commerce and fitness coaching business, both of which are brand new that he can now scale with such capital. Additionally, Cooper has access to the same investments I am in since he's a member of the Credit Stacking group, so Cooper is in a VERY good position to make a serious return on that $50K. Before we move on, I want to break down the steps on how we were able to help get him such a massive limit card:

1. Optimize personal credit profile
   1. Certain amount of personal accounts
   2. Low utilization
   3. Strong average-aged credit profile (with help of the AU strategy)
   4. Certain amount of collective personal limits
      1. We reached this by having him apply for two high-limit personal cards, one being the Chase Sapphire Preferred

Ensuring business was formed correctly

- Entity type
  a. Entity name
  b. Secretary of state updated with accurate business description

- Strategic relationship with the bank
  a. Previously having a personal credit card Chase Bank for the previous few months
  b. Business checking account at Chase with transaction activity

Properly submitting the credit application

- Applying through a Business Relationship Manager (who I personally introduced him to. I will dive deeper on what a Business Relationship Manager is in the next chapter)
  a. Properly selecting the business category and subcategories (more challenging and more important that someone who think)
  b. Strategically completing the personal income, rent payment, estimated business revenue, and estimated monthly spend sections (absolutely critical)

The combination of all these steps, which are all taught in very step-by-step detail in Credit Stacking, is the perfect recipe for a $50K 0-percent interest business credit card approval. And I almost forgot, this approval was on a business that was only nine months old and wasn't even making money! Many people think you need some super-aged and profitable business, but that is not true! The breakdown on the steps above is all you need to get access to $100K+ in 0-percent interest business credit (since you can do this on back-to-back cards over a variety of banks in a short period of time). At this exact time, you might not know the true impact of a business credit and how it differs from personal credit, so if that is you, that is okay; I will be covering that in a couple of chapters, and you may then realize how crazy getting approved for $100K in 0-percent interest business credit is. Ok, I'll spill the beans a little, but you can actually max out business cards, and since the account doesn't report to your personal credit, the utilization doesn't report, and it will not affect your personal credit score. We will go MUCH deeper in the business credit section and hang in there with me!

CREDIT MIX

Credit Mix is a much more simple section of your credit factor. This really only looks at the diversity you have on your credit report between different credit products, such as revolving (such as credit cards), auto loans, mortgages, installment loans, and student loans. Each of these types of loans are able to strengthen the Credit Mix section of your credit report. Revolving is the most popular credit card and easiest for someone to get so often; this holds 80 percent of the Credit Mix if not more, for the people that only have revolving accounts. In the eyes of the banks, someone is less risky if they have a diversified credit mix. For example, someone who has revolving, an auto loan, and a mortgage is less risky than someone who only has revolving accounts. However, this brings me to my next point, which is your debt-to-income ratio. A diversity in Credit Mix is helpful, but one thing to consider is your debt-to-income ratio, which essentially is a ratio of the debt you are borrowing relative to your income. If you are borrowing a lot but also making a lot, there is no issue here, but in the scenario someone is borrowing a lot but isn't reporting a lot of personal income, then this looks risky to the lenders (even with a diversified credit mix). When calculating your debt-to-income ratio (DTI), you will ideally want to be less than 36 percent. For example, if you have a balance of $40K that you owe to credit cards and an auto loan, and you are only reporting you make $100K, this would look risky, since that is a 40-percent DTI.

CASE STUDY

I learned about Credit Mix the hard way. When I applied for a recent Chase Business Ink card, I was only approved for $25K instead of my requested $50K (which is something you can do through Business

Relationship Managers). When I got the credit decision in the mail, it notified me of my limit and the reason the full request wasn't met. It stated the reason had something to do with my credit mix, and for a while, it had me thinking. I have exceptionally strong personal credit and very high personal credit card limits, so I knew it couldn't have been that specifically, but after really putting some thought into it, I realized it's because I only had revolving accounts reporting on my credit. I didn't have any auto loan, no student loan, no mortgage, no installment loan, only revolving accounts. I'm not saying to go out of your way to bring on more debt in the form of the credit products that I have just listed, but it's important to keep in mind that diversifying your credit mix could have a positive effect on your credit profile and ultimately help you get approved for more credit. Side note: I'm not an advocate of personal loans. They are very easy to get, but if you have sizable personal installment loans on your credit profile, it makes it more challenging to get approved for 0-percent interest business credit cards with sizable limits. I think good examples of personal installment loans would be financing any dental work, cosmetics procedures, something through PayPal credit, or anything else that reports as an installment loan but isn't for a crazy amount of debt. It's helpful to diversify your credit mix but to keep your DTI low.

NEW CREDIT

If you have ever been denied a credit card, one of the most popular credit card denial reasons that the bank will outline to you on the decision letter is "too many recently opened credit card accounts" or "too many recent hard inquiries." In the eyes of the lenders, if you are seeking tons of credit, and they can see this on your credit report from recently opened accounts or by having tons of recent inquiries, this is risky for them to lend to you. It's kind of interesting, but banks only want to lend money to people who don't need the money, as it's less risky to them. If they can see on your credit report that you are shopping around for credit from a variety of lenders, this makes it seem that you are more desperate to borrow money, and the banks do not like lending to people who seem desperate. You may not be desperate for money, but this is just how the banks see it if there is too much recent activity for new credit. In this section, there are very specific metrics that we want to stay under before applying for new credit accounts in terms of how many recent personal accounts you have opened in the last year, and also how many inquiries you have on each bureau prior to another application. Something that I strongly advocate to my Credit Stacking students is that you do not want to have more than four recently opened *personal* credit accounts before applying for another credit account. If you are over that number, you will have a very hard time getting approved for more. In terms of hard inquiries, I strongly advise against applying for more credit if your hard inquiries exceed two in a short period of time on any given bureau.

Out of the two scenarios I outlined above, one of them is far easier to fix than the other. If you have too many recently opened personal accounts, closing the accounts won't help at all since the opening date is still reported, but it's possible to actually delete the account from your credit file (this would close it and delete it). This isn't an easy option, though, and can take a few months through a credit repair professional. In terms of having too many hard inquiries, this is a much easier fix, which leads me into the next section on Credit Repair, but through disputing the inquiries, they are pretty simple to have removed from your credit report. Once they are removed, you should be in a much better position for future credit applications.

CREDIT REPAIR

This next part should actually be under the Payment History section, but it's such an important topic that I wanted to make it its own. Knowing how to make your score work for you looks like understanding these categories and working to cultivate a healthy score through them. It's likely that many people beginning this process are doing so with scores below 780, maybe even as low as 650 or 600. If this is you, you might be tempted to feel that this process will end with you realizing your credit is subpar and giving up on your dream of securing capital. I'm happy to tell you that this is far from true. There are so many business owners, self-starters, and entrepreneurs that have accomplished their goals from places of terrible credit and financial health. This is such a common story today that you do not need to worry. There are many steps that we can take to make sure your credit is up to where it needs to be. This process is called credit repair. It will consist of beginning with an in-depth look at your current credit health and disputing anything negative that is holding your score down. Fortunately for consumers in the United States, the Fair Credit Reporting Act (FCRA) has laws in place that protects consumers and allows them to dispute anything on their credit report that is unfair or inaccurate. What is incredible is that the burden of proof is on the creditors or bureaus and not you! Thanks to the FCRA, after something such as a late payment, collection, or bankruptcy is disputed, the creditors or bureaus have very little time to provide proof that the disputed derogatory mark is accurate and can verify that it was actually your fault. Based on the strict timelines that the FCRA gives to the creditors/bureaus and the incredibly common inaccuracies in their records, this makes it very effective for anyone to dispute any derogatory mark from their credit report.

I had one student who had a total of $21,000 in credit card debt that was sold to collections in addition to a car repossession. I connected him with our credit repair partner, who, within just under three months, was able to have the collections and repo cleared from his credit file! Because the FCRA is so protective of consumers, this, of course, is all done through a legal process and highly effective! Now, this individual has over a 700 credit score and has been able to get approved for credit cards, which was simply not possible before the derogatory items were disputed and cleared from his credit file.

Personal Credit

I want to emphasize, ANYTHING negative is disputable on your credit file. The burden of proof is on the creditors and bureaus, not you! It is possible to have any late payment, collection, charge-off, and most bankruptcies and repossessions removed! This is life-changing news to some that are dealing with <600 credit score. If this is you, just know that any credit score is fixable!

Additionally, similar strategies work just as effective with hard inquiries! Through very similar disputes, hard inquiries can be removed in as little as twenty-four hours or can take up to ~3 months, but through the right credit repair professional, each and every one can be successfully removed by law.

As I mentioned, we have a credit repair partner who provides this service to all Credit Stacking students (at industry low rates, I must add), and additionally, we provide step-by-step coaching on how to effectively go through the process yourself. This consists of letter templates to send to the creditors/bureaus, phone scripts, and timelines of it all so our students can clear their credit files of derogatory items themselves. We even have a specific phone script that gets hard inquiries removed in less than twenty-four hours, which is critical if you are trying to not lose any momentum through your credit card applications.

These steps will prove effective in a very short period of time for most. It may seem that it will take years, and for many, this is something that can be solved in only a matter of months. I can promise that in the end, your repaired credit will reap dividends that will accelerate you past a place of ever scoring that low again.

In the next chapter, we'll go into the actual cards and categories of cards themselves. With this groundwork laid, you'll be able to pick out and find all the capital that you need in a variety of business credit cards that I will lay out for you. Given the knowledge you've acquired in this chapter, it should not be too hard a learning curve, and by the end, you'll be able to maximize returns with low risk. Feel free to go back and review as much of the tips and tricks from this last chapter as you need, and remember, this book is your resource to obtain the capital that you need to make your dreams a reality. There will be sections that will pop for you more than other sections, but in the end, what matters is a strong understanding of the principles of credit stacking.

CHAPTER 3
CREDIT CARDS AND CALCULATED RISK

I knew that if I failed, I wouldn't regret that, but I knew the one thing I might regret is not trying.

Jeff Bezos

The story of Jeff Bezos is one that I've always thought really spoke to those of us willing to take risks. It goes that he analyzed the markets while working in an investment firm and saw that the internet was exploding in a way that many weren't taking advantage of. He took his family, moved out to the West Coast, and started his business, Amazon. It's a little-known website that, at the beginning, sold little things like books. This website went from small time retail to nationwide retail. It then expanded to selling more and more items. Eventually, the company was becoming so large that it started renting out server space, hosting server racks to businesses for off-site hosting, and providing other services for businesses. This is something fascinating about the business that many people don't know, that it makes a significant profit selling out server space for companies looking to host backups, full databases and websites, and data centers. It's a humongous operation now and one of the largest companies on earth. It's gone from a company started by an educated guess to a multinational hosting company, retailer, media company with its own studio productions that have won awards, and a delivery service that delivers at speeds that are unmatched by many shipping companies. The community of Amazon has built billions in revenue for thousands of people and has given small-time authors and producers places to sell their crafts and get their work out there to the public. Do you think that any of this would've happened if that calculated risk hadn't been taken? What if Bezos simply looked at his current job, which was a good job, there's no questioning it, and said, "Well, this is good enough. There's no way I'd take the risk and move out west." What would happen if he had just stayed where he was and not gone with his gut and his calculated risk?

So far, we've covered the principles of establishing good credit and making sure that you're in a good position to benefit optimally from Credit Stacking. This chapter is where we take that preparation and make it a reality. This is where we go from talk to action. I want you to be ready to go and take a risk or two. So many financial advisors make their money telling you to avoid credit cards and avoid any kind of debt for all time. And for many people, the steps in this book and my Credit Stacking Course may seem too risky. I don't want to discredit anyone who feels that the tips in this book are not for them. But I can promise you from my own career that these tips in here come from a place of calculated risk. There is no substitute for financial health and smart decisions with your finances, and we'll cover those principles heavily in this book too. At the core of this book is a desire to see your money work for you.

The truth is, there are billions available for businesses to use. The credit card system thrives off those who don't take care of their finances and who don't take control of their finances. Through the steps we're about to cover, you're going to drive yourself to the next level through smart, calculated business decisions.

This book is all about possibilities. Go through some of the steps with me and let me show how stacking your credit can work for you to help you gain control over your goals and dreams.

Our first step is to go over your scores and know what all you can apply for first.

After that, we'll cover what cards to apply for, when to apply for them, and how to do it.

And finally, this chapter will end with you understanding the specific fees you can waive, cards you can get, and credit lines that you can secure to get your money working for you.

So why credit?

Why not just use a standard debit account? It's a valid question. You could just use a debit account for your business like you do your own personal finances. Let's go over why I think you should use credit instead.

1. Protection
    1. Any fraudulent charges on your credit card will be reimbursed by the bank
    2. Ability to charge back on products and services
3. Rewards
    1. Points, points, points
    2. This is going to be a huge portion of the strategies we discuss that helps provide a major opportunity for free travel.

3. Card benefits
    - Top credit cards will include a variety of card benefits that ultimately give you free or discounted additional benefits to your life.
4. Relationship Building
    - Spending through a credit card will rapidly build trust with the lender, which will ultimately strengthen the foundation for ideal business credit card approval and limits.

PURCHASE PROTECTION:

Your card gives your protection? Well, if you ever have any fraudulent activity or any purchases that aren't fulfilled as promised, you can actually get a transaction completely erased from your statement and never have to pay for it. As a small business owner, this could come in handy if you purchase a good or service that simply doesn't function as promised or is a service that isn't delivered as agreed upon in your contract with them. This gives you the ability to keep your merchants accountable and keeping your purchases on credit cards protected and secure. Since this would give people more confidence with their spending on their credit cards, the banks are very helpful in these situations.

REWARDS:

If you are not already using credit cards for your purchases, you are missing out on thousands of dollars (if not tens of thousands of dollars) in free points or cash back per year. The points will make the difference between credit and debit for you. You are going to find in the coming chapters that the possibilities for using credit cards, especially if you are charging them for large business transactions and business expenses, is almost endless. You can easily transfer point balances to different accounts to 3X+ your points value, can redeem your points for cash or redeem your points through the travel portals for tons of free flights and hotels. Much of my full-time travel expenses on flights and hotels have been covered purely off of free credit card points!

CARD BENEFITS:

When it comes to the card benefits, it blows my mind on the additional free perks the banks give out by having the top cards. Things like $300 statement credits on travel, free airport lounge access, Lyft discounts, a statement credit for Global Entry/TSA Precheck, a statement credit for CLEAR (to skip airport lines), rental car status, hotel status, and a large variety of other free perks of credit cards help reduce costs in your life and ultimately provide a better experience for you.

RELATIONSHIP BUILDING:

One of the best ways to build a strong relationship with a bank before applying for business credit is to create a strong relationship with them on the personal side. To show spending and consistent on-time payment history will create strong trust with each lender. However, it's crucial that you have personal credit cards at banks that it's actually worth building a strong relationship to get the most value out of your efforts.

It's very clear that the benefits of using credit over debit are self-evident and easily usable if you simply know where to look and redeem the perks that they provide.

There's a catch, though. If you're used to simply using debit and cash payments, then you'll need to probably add protections between you and late fees. These are those annoying little things that like to jump out and grab unnecessary payments from you when you don't pay your balance in time. It's not too hard to protect against if you simply set up some safeguards.

First, it's important to understand what late fees I am referring to. If you don't pay your balance within thirty days, there will be a late payment notification that gets reported to the credit bureaus, but if you pay before thirty days is up, you will not have to worry about that penalty going out and being reported to the bureau. You may still have to pay the fees, but at least you won't have to worry about your credit score and potential borrowing power being affected, if you pay before thirty days.

The best tool in your arsenal is autopay. This option is offered by every credit card company and comes with no fee applied. All you have to do is go on to your credit card portal or account page and set up autopay with your debit account that is most likely to always have cash in it. Make sure that it's an account that won't be drained too easily, as you can still get an insufficient funds fee from your bank for using cash you don't have to pay off a credit card. An insufficient funds fee can set you back from future approval, so this is very important that this doesn't happen to you. Most autopay features have a way that you can adjust the frequency of payments to where you pay each statement, pay more than once a month, and so on. Depending on the account, it can also allow you to pay several days in advance or as close to the due date as you feel comfortable doing.

PERSONAL CREDIT CARDS

When it comes to making your next moves on personal credit, you will first want to start with awareness

If this doesn't make you comfortable yet, then the first product we'll discuss is a good first step to get you into the process of using a credit card. This first product is called a secured card. Simply put, a secured card is one that you have to load with money before using, so you aren't spending money that isn't there; you're spending money that is already loaded on to a card to be used. This cuts out the possibilities of late fees and derogatory marks to your credit account. With the use of this prepaid card, the process of building credit can be much easier for those who are more averse to the thought of using credit cards.

The rewards for these cards are a little less than a traditional credit card. But with their being just as easy, if not easier to be approved for, going ahead and signing up for one is a good step in the direction of getting your credit history started.

If you are brand new to credit or are rebuilding your credit history, I would strongly recommend you consider the secured credit cards at Bank of America and US Bank. This would only help you build credit history but also start to build relationships with these two top banks, which offer two of the best 0-percent interest business credit cards on the market.

WHAT TO APPLY FOR

I want to list some banks that offer great credit cards, in my opinion. Like we did in previous steps, we're going to focus on establishing history with a large, national bank with the best options and then work our way down the list. I want to also show you some awesome card options from each bank that you can use as a guide while applying through these banks. If I were to start from scratch, these are the cards I would focus on getting approved for. Not only for the benefits but to build strategic relationships that would set an incredible foundation for when I apply for business credit cards.

Note: before you apply to these cards, please make sure that you have the appropriate credit score as a rejection will not be very good for your credit. Also, please do not apply for them all at once, as you will see very poor results by doing so.*

Chase Freedom Unlimited

- $200 cash back sign up bonus
- 3X points on dining
- 3X points on drugstores
- 1.5X points on all other purchases
- 0% for 15 months
- No annual fee

Bank of America Cash Rewards

- $200 cash back sign up bonus
- 3% cash back in the category of your choice: gas, online shopping, dining, travel, drug stores, or home improvement/furnishings
- 0% for 15 months
- No annual fee

Credit Cards And Calculated Risk

American Express Marriott Bonvoy

- *75,000 Marriott Bonvoy points sign up bonus*
- *$200 statement credit at select US restaurants*
- *$300 statement credit to Marriott*
- *6X points on hotels*
- *3X points on dining and flights*
- *Complimentary Gold Status*
- *Airport lounge access*
- *$450 annual fee*

Chase Sapphire Reserve

- *50,000–100,000 sign up bonus*
- *$300 annual travel credit*
- *10X points on hotels and rental cars booked through chase.com*
- *3X points on travel and dining*
- *50% bonus on points when redeeming through chase.com*
- *Global Entry and TSA Precheck credit ($100 value)*
- *Complimentary airport lounge access*
- *No foreign transaction fee*
- *$550 annual fee (but waivable through a secret taught in the Credit Stacking program)*

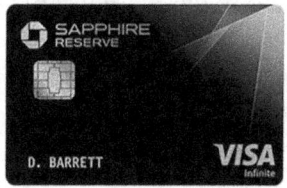

US Bank Altitude Connect

- 5X points on hotels and car rental booked through USbank.com
- 4X points on travel and gas stations
- 2X at grocery stores and dining
- $30 annual credit on streaming services such as Netflix, Apple TV, and Spotify
- Global Entry and TSA Precheck credit ($100 value)
- No foreign transaction fee
- Cell phone protection
- No annual fee for first year

These are just a few of the top banks that I highly recommend for quality cards up front. As time goes on, we'll explore more than just consumer cards and will get into more elite cards and services offered with greater and greater benefits. Each card with these banks will have their own unique perks that help you achieve different goals. Some are better for travel, some get better cash back on gas, and all of them can be assets for you while you credit stack toward financial freedom.

There are some great products available at each bank. I want to go over as many as I can with you, but given that there's only so much you can get from reading about the subject, I want to encourage you to sign up for my Credit Stacking mentorship, where I can walk you through several of the cards with their own unique perks and features, which will ultimately help you receive more value to your life.

Credit Cards And Calculated Risk

We'll go through the steps of signing up for these cards and some great strategies for optimizing your returns from them.

Well, so far, the few options we've viewed here could already boost your projects and capital in new directions. And there are tons of additional cards that we just don't have the room to list here. But what about cards that you want to avoid?

From my experience, there is no reason you should ever need a Capital One Card. I have no personal problem with the bank or anything like that, I promise you, but when you hear my reason, you'll understand. Capital One pulls from all three bureaus. That, alone, is a reason to avoid the card since receiving a triple pull will dramatically slow down your journey in credit. But it also really doesn't benefit you in the long term to establish a relationship with this bank either. There are much better options, and why waste a hard inquiry when it can go to a better option. Additionally, most of their business credit cards report to your personal credit profile, which completely defeats the purpose of it being a business card!

When it comes to building relationships with banks, I only think it makes sense to build with banks who have business credit cards, and I mean good business cards. Banks that don't offer good business cards I avoid spending my time on building a relaZtionship with. Other notable banks that I avoid are Discover since their cards are very elementary, and the business cards generally report to your personal credit profile, which, again, defeats the purpose of it being a business card.

Understanding **what** to apply for, **when** to apply, and **how** to apply is crucial to maximize the results on approvals and limits you receive on your credit applications.

We briefly touched on what to apply for above, but these questions are to help you maximize the amount of value you are able to add to your life:

- Do you have a travel card yet?
- What size of limits do you already have?
- What banks do you have the best relationship with?
- What banks are you looking to build a relationship with?
- What bureau do you have the least amount of hard inquiries on?
- What cards give you the highest limits?

Ultimately, these questions will help you choose the best cards to apply for to not only add more value to your life but to also create a very strong personal credit foundation. The stronger the foundation is, the more success you will see on business card approvals and limits.

WHEN TO APPLY

After deciding what personal card(s) you are going to apply for, the next step is to understand when to apply for them. The questions below will help guide you finding that answer:

How many personal credit accounts have you opened in the last six and twelve months?

- *How many hard inquiries do you have on each bureau in the last six and twelve months?*
- *What is your utilization on each personal credit card account?*
- *What state do you live in?*
- *At what banks are you applying for cards?*

The reason I ask these questions is that based on these answers, it could point to when you should be applying. Jumping the gun on card applications without a plan in place can easily jeopardize your approvals and waste your time.

After you've answered those questions, this also brings us to a good point to cover early on. While you're going and applying for cards, make sure that you know which bureau your bank pulls from. The approval process is going to differ if, for example, you've applied for three cards through Experian, but you're trying to apply for another one. In this situation, it may be more beneficial to apply for a card through a bank that uses a different credit bureau to run their hard inquiries. When banks pull your credit upon applying for a credit card, each bank can choose either one, two, or all three bureaus. Each bank has their own preference on which bureau(s) they pull from, and what makes it confusing is that this can change based on your location. For example, In Washington State, Bank of America may pull from Transunion, but in California, they may pull from Experian. We actually have an inhouse database with thousands of data points in Credit Stacking to ensure the research is accurately provided to give out students the highest chance of success on their approvals while maximizing the amount of cards they can be approved for, but this information isn't difficult for you and others who have recently submitted credit applications.

Some common examples of a bank and the bureau that they pull their hard inquiries from are:

- Bank of the West – Experian
- Barclays – Transunion
- American Express – Experian
- KeyBank – Equifax
- BB&T – Equifax (sometimes Experian)
- Alliant – Equifax
- Bank of America – Experian or Transunion
- FNBO – Experian

You can use your knowledge of which bureaus will be pulled from to avoid flooding one or more bureaus with your applications and their hard inquiries. You don't want that, trust me. This is some secret sauce, but with accurate bank/bureau credit pull data points, you can give yourself the highest chance of an approved credit application with a favorable limit at a rapid pace.

Now that you have a good idea on **what** to apply for and **when** to apply for each card, we need to look at any specific instructions on **how** to apply for different cards.

HOW TO APPLY

The first thing you need to understand in the application process is that depending on the bank, there is a different ideal way to apply for their credit cards to give you the highest chance of an approval (and ideally with a very high limit). Since credit card fraud is exceptionally high, online application processes have the lowest approval odds. However, if you know that you'll most likely be approved for a credit card, then go ahead. But if there is any doubt for you, I'd go ahead and make an appointment to go and apply in the local branch of that bank. Online applications seem great, and if you have a great relationship with the bank and strong credit, oftentimes there isn't an issue. Just make sure that you give yourself every reason to be successful here.

Now that we've covered the build-up to this next step, we can discuss actually applying for your first cards. This is the fun part. I'm of the mindset to be positive yet realistic, as this is crucial to getting back-to-back approvals Credit Stacking students frequently see. You can easily find cards to meet your needs but need to make sure you're ensuring an approval. Use the knowledge you have, but keep the positivity. Remember, we promised to keep a mindset of "can do" rather than "best to just not even try." You've got to keep it realistically positive to get optimal results from this step.

You'll want to look up your preferred card, be optimistic on the reported income, and make sure that your information is completely accurate. When it comes to reported income, this is more like an honor system than anything else since there are only a select few of the top banks who actually verify. On your personal information, such as address and social security number, one small mistake will jeopardize the entire application. Once everything looks good, then submit!

When it comes to the credit decision on personal credit cards, oftentimes it's instant approval, but sometimes you will see it go to a pending or even denied status. If it goes pending or denied, it might not be over yet. For a "pending" application, this is generally just the need to verify information on your application and necessary to go to the underwriting team. If this is the case, call the bank and let them know you just applied, and ask them if you can provide any additional information to them to approve your application. If done properly, this often leads to an approval. For denied applications, you probably didn't know this, but you can immediately contact that bank through the bank reconsideration line and request a reconsideration of the credit decision. If there are things on your application they didn't like, you can discuss it with them and see what you can clear up to make it more attractive to the bank in question. It is definitely an incredible hack that is overlooked. In Credit Stacking, we never leave the possibility of an approval on the table!

RECONSIDERATION

This process of reconsideration requires promptness, politeness, and persistence.

Promptness:

You want to call immediately after the rejection. Don't give it time to sit around for too long. Remember, this needs to go away quickly so that you can have a good approval record, and the longer you wait jeopardizes the need for the bank to pull your credit again (giving you another hard inquiry). After a credit card denial, you will often have to wait three to six months to re-apply on the same card, so it is best to get it done promptly.

Politeness:

When you call, it's important to be polite to give yourself the best shot of approval. The phone representatives deal with so many angry and unpleasant customers, so it's important to be pleasant for them to comply with your request. Additionally, you will want to be sharp and act professionally. Go through the conversation in your head beforehand, know your information accurately, and be prepared for the call. If they need to verify any information with you, and you are not accurate with providing it, then your chance of approval dramatically decreases. I like to write my information down in front of me beforehand, such as my reported income, monthly rent payment amount, and any other personal information that you want to have handy to ensure you sharply provide it to them.

Persistence:

If the representative tells you that they can't help you get approved, take them for their word, thank them for their time, and hang up . . .

And then call immediately back to the same number.

If your first call is unsuccessful, you want to call a few more times, each as if it is your first. I'm not saying you should lie, but just act like the first call didn't happen. You will want to emphasize how important it is to maintain a positive relationship with the bank, that you love the specific bank, and explain how perfect the card will be for you based on the upcoming expenses you have coming up (moving, planning a wedding or event, renovating your kitchen, etc.).

This step can be a little difficult as it feels like it shouldn't really be allowed to happen, but the beauty is it is completely doable and even has its own process.

I want to give you some phone numbers to help kickstart this process for you. These are the numbers you'll call for the different banks. Remember, this step is basically the best weapon in your arsenal to help you fight for a great credit record. As these numbers may change over time, it might be best to also Google "[name of bank] reconsideration phone number" to make sure you have the correct phone number.

- American Express
    - 877-399-3083 for new accounts
    - 866-314-0237 for existing account holders
- Bank of America
    - Personal cards: 866-505-7481
    - Business cards: 888-782-7717
    - Chase Bank
- Personal cards: 888-270-2127
    - Business cards: 800-453-9719

These are just a few of the numbers for the big banks. We go through a lot of coaching for this process in the Credit Stacking mentorship, as there are so many tips and different specific scripts that can get you in the door. Additionally, we have a database of reconsideration phone numbers to every bank, even the smaller ones that don't publicly post their reconsideration phone number online. But to start, the top three banks above will put you on a great start to getting access to more capital.

At this point, you should have a good understanding of how exactly to create a personal credit profile that acts as a strong foundation and makes you much more attractive to the banks. Not only are you more attractive to banks now, which will leads to future 0-percent interest business credit cards approvals, but now you'll have some of the top personal credit cards, which give you spending power, free benefits that comes with each card, and incredible rewards based on each dollar that is strategically spent through these cards that will provide cash back savings and loads of free travel.

Once you've gotten this far, it's hardly a stretch to say that you could even turbo charge your credit limits just a little bit more: credit line increases.

ADDITIONAL BENEFITS

Before we close this chapter out, I want to highlight two additional ways to receive even more benefits from your cards.

There really is no end to the perks and advantages of utilizing credit for yourself. You just need to know where to look. The strategy of credit stacking is one with a lot of numbers, figures, phone calls, meetings, and new information that is changed on a regular basis, so I really want to extend an invitation to you to help with this area of the process. If you join my community on the Credit Stacking Course and the Facebook network that we've been creating, I can promise you a group of like-minded individuals, myself included, will be there to help you through the entire process. It's hard to get up-to-date information unless you are surrounding yourself with a network of others who are also credit stacking. This can only help you get one step ahead in the process.

The world of credit doesn't stop in this chapter with personal credit cards. There are so many categories of business credit and corporate credit that we haven't even touched on yet. And the section on travel takes you places this chapter barely scratched the surface of. It extends to many more products that we'll discuss in the following chapters and has so many perks that I highly doubt you'll be able to take advantage of all of them. But, then again, it doesn't hurt you to try.

CHAPTER 4

USING BUSINESS CREDIT TO GAIN MOMENTUM

The harder I work, the luckier I get. When you have momentum going, play the momentum.

Donald Trump

The key in business is to get momentum going. It's often said that to do this, you need to be lucky, that you must just be in the right place at the right time. While there is something to be said for putting yourself in the position to be more fortunate in your interactions, your business is going to run on the momentum that you create. You can network and surround yourself with like-minded business owners and high performers to increase your chances of success, but at the end of the day, the difference is going to be made by the value of your company and the momentum it creates. In this chapter, we'll be looking at how your business can accelerate its momentum with business credit. The credit that we've already reviewed is mostly at a consumer level. While many of the same rules apply to both consumer and business credit, there are several different technical aspects that you need to understand. Our first part of this chapter will cover the different methods of financing a business venture and how to make sure that your credit works well for you through this process. After that, we'll go over the process of getting cash from your cards and using a liquidation method to make your cards work even better for you. By the end of this chapter, you'll have a better understanding of how to make your own luck by raising adequate capital.

I want to start off by saying that this book is for anyone looking to start a business, expand a business, or simply take control of their finances. The business aspect of this chapter, however, does mean that it will mostly deal with business credit-related terms and topics. I would still encourage you to read it, though. Who knows, that plan you always had but didn't assume the risk for might suddenly become a reality for you.

Let's start by reviewing how you could go about funding your business. There are some standard methods that involve raising your own cash and using it as your starting capital. If that doesn't sound risky to you, it should. The problem there is that you're footing 100 percent of the risk. You don't stand to gain anything if this idea goes south, and then you're left with nothing to show.

You could receive a business loan, but then you'd be paying high interest rates on a lump sum of debt that you can't transfer elsewhere.

You could incorporate a partner. This idea isn't a bad one at all. There are so many things a business partner can do for you. The problem is that you aren't going to own your business in entirety and will end up with a large portion of your business shared with another partner.

And then you could use a 0-percent interest business credit card, or several cards, using banking relationships to keep your standing good and keep yourself always just one application away from more business credit.

If you noticed a slight bias there, it's because my favorite method is the last one. Leave your cash for your long-term investments like your retirement, portfolio, home, and all those long-term assets. Use your credit to fund the areas in your life that may leave you liable. As we'll discuss in more and more detail, business credit can definitely work to deliver those results you'd get from the other methods with much less risk.

The key difference that we have to notate before going forward is that your business credit is an entirely different beast from your personal credit. You aren't going to see your business's credit on your FICO score, and it will be assessed using different metrics than your FICO score. I need to make that distinction now because the usage of personal credit cards for raising business capital is not a great idea. Sure, the process we've gone through has been personal credit heavy up to this point. That will come in handy later. But for now, we need to focus on securing your business credit using the methods necessary to impress the credit bureaus that are responsible for reporting your business activities and rating your business credit score.

The next step we'll need to cover is the process of how to get you in the right place to get approved for business credit cards. This is going to help you fund your business, consolidate debt, and possibly even invest your money in business expansion.

BUSINESS ENTITY SET UP

In addition to knowing the terms that you'll hear in Credit Stacking, it is also important to understand that not all businesses are viewed the same by banks and lenders. The North American Industry Classification System, or NAICS, has codes that can be found on their website that define a business based on the activities in which they predominantly engage. Each business category is assigned a SIC Code (Standard Industrial Classification) which can be found on an SIC Code search website. This is important to understand because, based on your SIC code, you could be ineligible for business credit. An example of such an industry would be a travel agency or an auto dealer. Both business categories are determined to be high risk by their NAICS code and would have reduced chances for ideal approvals on business credit applications. In the glossary, where the terms and definitions are listed, you'll find a more complete list of industries that are either automatic rejections or potentially high-risk industries (subject to stricter underwriting guidelines). What this means for you, the business owner, is that to maximize your capital raising efforts, you may need to consider establishing your business under a category that puts it at a better chance for credit approval. This can look like establishing your real estate business as a consulting firm that deals in real estate as well, or even start a brand new "consulting business." Another tip is if you have an existing business, you may need to make sure that business is under a business name that doesn't directly address that you may deal in these categories that are at a higher risk for rejection. For example, if you are in the credit space, a business name such as "JM Consulting" would have dramatically better results than "JM Credit Repair." When it comes to a business name, I tend to go on the vague side to keep it simple and reduce risk. There is always a workaround; the main thing is you need to have a narrative that fits your business in a low-risk NAICS category so you can maximize your funding results.

This caution around your business's designation may seem like a small detail before we begin our discussion of credit stacking. But it is incredibly important to set up your business with maximum fundability from the beginning like this. The process of setting up (or optimizing) your entity, while not very difficult, is explained much better in my Credit Stacking course through screen shares and detailed step-by-step instructions, but let me dive into three things where you need to make sure you have the right information properly entered. The first is on Dun & Bradstreet (DNB), which is a business credit bureau that banks will also pull from (which is separate from your personal credit reports). On your business's DNB profile, there will be a place to accurately add your NAICS code. You will want to make sure this aligns with your low-risk narrative of business operations. If Dun & Bradstreet doesn't sound familiar to you, there is still a decent chance a profile was automatically made for you, I still advise to search on DNB under their "DUNS look up" feature to see if you have a profile. If you don't, I would make one. Secondly, you will want to make sure your NAICS code is accurately inputted on your bank account. This is best to do right from the beginning when you open up your account. I normally give the code to the banker to have confidence they don't mess it up, as this could have a dramatic effect on funding results. Lastly, on the Secretary of State website, you will want to make sure your business description is accurate. If you check off these three things, you will be in a much better place and increase the fundability for your business.

BANKING RELATIONSHIPS

The first step in the process of building your credit is a strong relationship with a good bank. It's not opening a random card or taking out a random loan. The highest yield approach is to start and maintain a strong relationship where you can potentially go for your current and future business credit needs. While there are many good options for this step, I would highly recommend you make Chase Bank your first stop. Establishing credit with Chase Bank has seen better success than others, in my experience. If you prefer another top bank like Bank of America or US Bank, that is fine and should yield similar results.

There is a full stop needed here: Only build a relationship with a bank that offers 0-percent interest business credit cards.

There is no need for you to waste time and effort on a bank that will not deliver what you need in the end. As I already know Chase has that kind of card available, I can safely say it will be a good option. There are several grade-A banks that can deliver the results you need, but to do so, they have to offer a 0-percent interest business credit card. Once you find a grade-A bank that has that option, you can go ahead and work on the process of establishing a relationship with that bank. This relationship will foster the growth that you need much quicker and more effectively than simply applying through online promotions.

This process revolves around the relationship you will establish with that bank. As it will be a business credit card you'll be after, you'll want to open a business checking account first. I cannot emphasize enough to you how important it is to open a business checking account at your choice of top bank before ever trying to apply for credit there. It will help if you have already established a few years of consistent banking through that business account there too. The goal is to leverage their trust in you to get access to more of their money. This begins with opening the checking account we mentioned with at least one major bank. Now that you've gotten that account opened, you can accelerate your growth by opening at least one business account at a regional bank or even a credit union. The more accounts that you can open for your business's capital, the better leverage you'll have when you apply for your business credit cards.

A note to keep in mind is that if you already have an account open, say at a local or regional bank, it's no issue. Just go ahead and open one with a national bank and see if you can move some of your business's capital to that bank account, and I can promise you it won't hurt you down the road. Now that you've got your accounts set up, you can start to transfer capital that is related to your business. You don't need to do much with this capital. Just keep it moved strictly between your accounts at the national bank and the regional bank, and you'll see over time that it will work to give you a good standing with that bank. Banks want that money there. It stands in their best interest to keep you as the customer happy and to keep your money from your business in their bank. This is where that relationship will come from. Being a loyal customer of their bank will create a client relationship that will stand to help you develop a good credit standing with them.

Now that you've gotten your credit history working for you, I want to stop and look at the actual process that goes into calculating your credit score. As we discussed earlier, you're going to be rated by three different agencies for your credit score. This process will determine, for banks and potential lenders, whether you're a risky or safe bet. Your credit score will be assessed by two major companies, FICO and VantageScore. As you may already know, if you've ever had credit accounts, your credit score can make or break your chances of getting a loan, mortgage, or credit card. Ideally, you want a score somewhere above 780. This would categorize you as having excellent credit. Anything below that may need to be a score you want to raise for optimal results.

You'll want to start by setting up a business checking account for yourself. There are several different products, but once again, I'd say go straight for the big-ticket bank and get a Chase business debit account. In my experience, starting at the top like that just nets you more in the long run.

You'll need to start this process out clean, no derogatory marks, no more than one late payment, and with four to five accounts that are at least three months old. With this kind of a history being necessary, you'll want to exercise extreme caution to get your accounts to this kind of footing.

HOW TO FINANCE A BUSINESS

When you are looking to turn a business idea into a tangible business, the first step is always figuring out how to fund it. In terms of acquiring the necessary funding, there are a variety of options that are available to you, some more common than others. Over the last decade as an entrepreneur, I have studied each option thoroughly and have personal experience with each of the funding options I am about to outline. Each has its pros and cons, but one of them is a clear winner, in my opinion, with the most pros and least cons. When I am considering each option, I am essentially evaluating the risk vs. reward and considering how each will give me the highest chance of success.

SELF-FUNDING

For most people, starting a business or funding an investment starts out of their own pocket, using your hard-earned cash to finance 100 percent of the business. This is exactly what I did for my first variety of businesses, such as my Hoverboard business (Glidr) and my inflatable lounger business (Dumbo Lounge Sacks). For most young entrepreneurs, this can be extremely challenging to manage with such limited personal savings to allocate to your business idea, and it certainly was for me at the time. When my partner and I at the time had the idea, it was our go-to idea to fund the new business bank account with some personal savings so we could have some working capital to start growing the new business. See, for most people, this is also the go-to option, as it seems like common sense if you want to start something. For us, we each had very little personal savings, so it didn't allow us to fund much into the business bank account for working capital. In a business like this, we had to invest our money into inventory for the product to arrive, run ads, or book event space to sell the items, and then reinvest the proceeds into more inventory and then do it all again. It was a process that was working for us, but a very slow one.

I'm not sure if you remember, but hoverboards became extremely popular, mainly within a time frame of one year. Fortunately for my business partner and I, we were on the front lines of this trend and became one of the first US-based brands to import these and sell them in the state. We were buying them for ~$400 and selling them for $1,200; it was insane. I truly think we could have made 10X the amount of money we made if only we had more working capital from the beginning. But again, at the time self-funding the business was the only option we knew! We thought this is how everyone did it. At times, it was discouraging because we would notice how fast other entrepreneurs were able to scale, but we stuck to our grind.

At the end of the day, I'm a big believer in putting your hard-earned cash and personal savings into long-term investments like stocks, real estate, or crypto. There are many other options on funding a business that I'm about to dive into, and I think after reading through them, you would probably also start to agree with me.

EQUITY PARTNER

Once my partner and I were able to successfully launch Glidr and show some good progress, this led us into learning about the second way to fund a business, which was through an equity partner. At this point, we actually pitched our business idea to a group of high-level social media influencers, who, in trade for equity, gave us cash for working capital to grow the business. This was great because it was firstly reducing our risk since we didn't have to pour more of our savings into the business to grow it but also because it gave us the opportunity to scale faster since we had more cash to work with. At this point, we felt pretty smart since we found a new way to finance a business that gave us a couple great benefits. This option could be effective for many entrepreneurs but also brings its risks. The first is control. Once you are giving away equity you could also be giving away voting rights and control on the business, which could limit your vision on the business if you are not able to conduct business as you see it best fit. The second is paying out distributions. Once you have equity partners, you are now sharing the proceeds with your new partners. This could be a great thing if they are bringing massive value to the table, but in the scenario when they are not bringing as much value as you originally anticipated, then it could bring some animosity, but you are still obligated to pay them out based on their equity percentage.

When I reflect back on my experience in the Dumbo Lounge Sacks business venture, it reminds me of another experience I would like to share about equity partners. This was a rapidly growing business, and it actually caught a lot of attention from outside investors in efforts to get involved. We ended up in negotiations with two extremely wealthy individuals (one of them a daughter of a hundred millionaire), which leads to a pretty interesting situation. She and her partner approached us and essentially promised many things, but to list a few: help us order more inventory in bulk upfront, bring our production price down, get us vendor space at the best music festivals, and land us big licensing deals with companies to do custom orders. This was the best news we had ever heard! We thought we were going to become millionaires! So we decided this was the best option for us, which led to us signing the agreement and opening up a joint bank account. One thing I might add is that such a deal required my partner and I to give up control of decisions and controller power over the bank account. If all the promises were delivered, this was a no brainer for us; however, many of the promises fell through. To make a long story short, it didn't work out, and we made the decision to buy them out months later, which was not easy. Looking back, I am actually super grateful for the opportunity since it taught us so much. Ultimately, we could have negotiated harder and most importantly executed an agreement that outlined each and every one of their promises so we could hold them accountable, which, unfortunately, we were too naive and failed to do. But, hey, that's business, or anything in life; you live and you learn!

Through this route of funding a business, it's crucial you are bringing on the right partner and have very strong and clear agreements of what is expected from each party to ensure the success of the business and that each party feels good about the partnership. The last thing you want to do is give control or profits away to someone who you prefer not to. Even if you keep a majority stake over an equity partner, I have had other examples where it can be annoying them breathing over your shoulder as you are making decisions for the business.

BUSINESS LOAN

The third way to finance a business is through a business loan. This can be a decent way to finance a business if you have exhausted all other options, but the main reason I wouldn't prefer to go this route is because these types of loans require you to pay interest. Especially if you are launching a new business without the ability to show cash flow or bank statements, the rates for business loans are often in the double digits. Anytime you are paying interest on borrowed money, it just makes succeeding in business that much harder since you now have to factor the paid interest into your profit margins. If you have a business with documentation, you can provide to the banks to show its cash flow and two years of age (and have good credit); you have the ability to find single digits rates, but still at the end of day, you are paying interest on the borrowed money, which, after I lead into the fourth option of how to finance a business or investment, you would probably agree it doesn't make the most sense. I have personally gone through the steps to see my business loan options on two of my businesses, and I wasn't able to find something that was super incentivizing just based on the terms of the loan compared to my other options.

CREDIT STACKING

During my travel company business venture (Sendit Cabo), we weren't able to get approved for any reasonable business loans from the banks due to the age of our business and our thin personal credit reports, but we were able to land a loan from a family member. Through this route, we were able to borrow $50,000 to purchase hotel inventory, but it came at a cost of 10-percent APR to borrow it. So over a year, it would cost us $5,000 to float the $50,000 balance. With our limited knowledge at the time in 2016, this was our only option of borrowing, so we had to take it for us to scale the way we wanted to. The following twelve months were an incredibly eventful time for my partner and me with where the business brought us. Sendit Cabo was a collegiate travel company where we specialized in organizing travel experiences for college students, our three biggest events being Cabo Spring Break, Whistler College Weekend, and yacht parties in Seattle. From our first year in business to our second, we had very slow growth, and this was really due to our cash holdings at the time. The business model we had for our travel company consisted of buying up timeshare contracts in bulk at top tier resorts, and this required a lot of up-front cash. Another way to go about the business was to work directly with the hotels (vs. through timeshare contracts), which would have helped by only requiring a deposit down on the rooms; however, the timeshare model gave us incredibly higher margins, which allowed a small company like us to compete with our competitors the best we could. From year two to year three, it really got good, and this is where the $50,000 loan came in. One thing we realized is that as we were scaling up, we needed more hotel inventory, and we needed it fast to be able to accommodate the demand we were receiving from our west coast campus tour. When it came to allocating the $50K, we didn't even question where to spend it; we knew that buying up inventory would give us the best chance in taking market share from our competitor. I'm going to shorten up the rest of the story for you to save some time and get to the point, but essentially there were three big events that followed. The first was the US government issued a level three travel advisory to the state of Baja California Sur (the Mexican state that Cabo

San Lucas is in that we were selling trips to) after there was some recent gang violence, which advised to "reconsider travel." This was all over the news and made it very challenging to sell any of the inventory we just invested the $50K (and more) into. Secondly, fast forward a couple of months of sixteen-hour workdays, the largest student travel company in the country, and our number-one competitor, JusCollege, reached out to us in an effort to acquire our business. This was incredibly out of the blue and a major change of pace with JusCollege since all previous communication was extremely competitive up to this point. A couple of months through a variety of meetings, reviewing financials, and negotiating the offer, we came to an agreement to sell the businesses for a six-figure acquisition! We also learned through their pitch that at the same time JusCollege was acquiring us, they were getting acquired by Pollen, a UK tech and events startup who just raised over $60 million to expand into the United States. This was an incredible accomplishment for us, and we were so stoked! And for the third point I mentioned there was, before the acquisition date in March 2020, we ended up selling out of all our hotel inventory prior to the trips even with the travel advisory setback! The six-month period leading up to the acquisition was an incredibly challenging time for us, but fortunately quite rewarding on our exit. The biggest lesson I learned from the business venture is that having more working capital in a business gives you the ability to scale faster and ultimately a higher chance to succeed. The loan was a key factor in helping us take enough market share from our competitor, which sparked initial interest from them to reach out in an effort to acquire us. Without the loan and speed we gained, I'm not sure if the acquisition would have been offered to us. This was my first experience on a business loan, and wow did it open my eyes to what is possible in scaling a business.

0-PERCENT INTEREST BUSINESS CREDIT

Finally, to the fourth way to finance a business or investment, 0-percent interest business credit! After almost a decade in business and exploring all options on the market, I have found that funding something using 0-percent interest business credit has the most clear advantages. Through this method, you are able to pay no more for the loan (borrowing for free), it gives you more of an ability to keep all the equity, profit, and control, and you are able to secure hundreds of thousands in funding while keeping your personal credit score high, which gives you the ability to keep seeking more of it! This is precisely what I have been doing to fund multiple businesses or investments over the last two years since I was approved for my first business credit card in April 2020. I found this to be the easiest and most effective way to borrow money in a short period of time. What blew my mind is that I've been an entrepreneur since 2013, and I just recently learned about taking advantage of this method in 2020! I can only imagine how more successful in business I would have been if I learned what I'm teaching you in this book when I was eighteen, just graduating high school before I started any of my businesses or investing.

Since learning about business credit in 2020, I felt like I have been at a disadvantage in business my whole life up until this point. From then on, I made it my mission to help other entrepreneurs with this same information that allowed me to get approved for ~$500K in credit in just a fourteen-month period. I have a variety of success stories I could share about students, but the ones that really stick out to me are the students of mine who have recently graduated college and have seen incredible success. The first is Cooper, who was a recent graduate of University of Arizona. Within just a few months of working together, I was able to help him get approved for his first business credit card at Chase for a $50,000 approval! This was on the Chase Business Ink Unlimited, which gave him the $50,000 at 0-percent interest for twelve months, which allowed him to start an e-commerce store and make a couple of other investments that now provide him monthly passive income. The second is Loren, a twenty-three-year-old guy who just graduated from Arizona State University. Within the first year, he was able to get approved for $101,000 of business credit, $80,000 of it being approved at 0-percent interest. He then also started an e-commerce store and got involved in Airbnb short-term rentals and a variety of other investments that are making him monthly passive income—at age twenty-three! I'm super excited for him. Oftentimes, we are seeing results like this much faster, but since these gentlemen were a bit younger and newer to credit, we had to spend time optimizing their personal credit first. Regardless, can you imagine being that old and having such access to capital? When I was graduating college, I think I had $10K to my name, and that is how I would finance my business ideas. No wonder I felt like other entrepreneurs had an advantage because they did! And that advantage was 0-percent interest business credit.

BUSINESS CREDIT

At this point, you have probably read the words "business credit" a thousand times, but now it's time to really dive into the details so you can best understand the power of it and start using it as a tool to massively accelerate financial freedom. Before going into my favorite business credit cards and how to effectively apply for them, I first want to cover the basics of what exactly is business credit, what are the benefits, what can you actually use business credit for, and what requirements you should meet before submitting any business credit applications.

WHAT IS BUSINESS CREDIT?

Business credit is a way for you to borrow money from banks by leveraging your Employer Identification Number (EIN) rather than just your social security number (SSN). This gives you the ability to take advantage of the strengths of your business, such as entity type, entity age, business banking relationship, and estimated revenue instead of only your reported personal income. Business credit card limits are often much higher than personal limits, which gives you even more spending power and ability to start a business, scale a business, or fund an investment. Technically, it's possible to apply for a business card through your SSN as a sole proprietor; however, I highly recommend you submit your applications with some more of a business structure, such as an LLC or Corporation. If you do not have an LLC or Corporation yet, I recommend filing one. Even if you don't plan on using it immediately, there is value to letting it age.

BENEFITS OF BUSINESS CREDIT

When it comes to business credit, there are incredible benefits that outweigh the benefits of using personal credit in business and investing. It's a whole other beast that only the highly educated are knowledgeable about, and fortunately for you reading this book right now, you are going to learn how to use it as a tool to your advantage. The first major benefit of business credit is the fact that business credit accounts do not report to your personal credit report. Essentially what this means is that once you are approved for a business credit account, you won't actually see the account show up on your personal credit when you check your report like your other personal accounts do. This is absolutely massive for a few key reasons.

The first is that since the account doesn't report, that means other banks cannot see other business credit card accounts. For example, if you were approved for a $30,000 American Express (Amex) card, when you apply for business cards at Chase, US Bank, or any other banks, these other banks cannot see that American Express is lending you $30,000. This is because the Amex card is a business card, and the account simply does not report to your personal credit.

Secondly, since the account does not report, lenders are not able to see the opening date of the account like they can on personal cards. As we previously went over in personal credit, if you have too many recently opened personal credit accounts, you look risky to future lenders. However, since the business credit account and its opening date isn't reporting, they can't see your recently opened business credit account. This gives you the ability to apply for a large variety of business cards in the same day, month, or year. The only thing that limits your speed is the amount of hard inquiries at the time of each application, but that leads me to my next point.

Thirdly, because the business credit account isn't reporting to your personal credit report, this gives you the ability to dispute hard inquiries to get them removed. See, on open personal accounts, if you dispute the hard inquiry associated with the opening of that credit account, it can risk the closure of the account; however, since the business credit account doesn't report, when you dispute the hard inquiry associated with the opening of the account, that cannot trace it back to an open account (because the business account isn't reporting to your personal credit report!). This is incredibly massive and allows individuals like myself and everyone in the Credit Stacking program to move very quickly through their credit journey. By using this strategy, you are able to go through four "Credit Stacks" (rounds of applications) per year rather than just two like a normal person would be doing if they didn't know this was possible. The process of removing a hard inquiry associated with the opening of the business account is a whole other topic, but just know it's doable and a major key of how I was able to get approved for ~$500,000 in credit in a fourteen-month period. The specific strategy is outlined in detail for our Credit Stacking members who are also seeing similar success in their first year of credit stacking.

Lastly, since the business account isn't reporting at all, what does that mean for the accounts utilization? What happens to your credit score after you max out a 0-percent interest business credit card and leave a balance month after month? If you guessed "nothing," you're right! Since the account doesn't report, the utilization doesn't report either! This now gives you the ability to not only get approved for a large variety of 0-percent interest business credit cards but to also max them out and leave a balance through the 0-percent interest introductory period without it affecting your personal credit score at all. Brilliant, right?! When I first learned this, it completely rocked my world and was one of the main drivers for me to seek more and more credit. Imagine what you can do in business or investing after getting approved for $100K+ of 0-percent interest credit while having your personal credit score untouched and the ability to get more credit as you go? For most entrepreneurs, this is absolutely life-changing and is exactly what's happening for Credit Stacking members on a weekly basis. One more thing I want to add is the importance of only using business credit cards for your business or investments, rather than any personal credit cards. Since utilization on only personal credit cards affects your credit, this makes it extremely risky to use personal credit cards for any business expenses or investment. In the scenario that the business or investment doesn't provide the necessary cash flow or returns to pay off the balance, it would leave your personal credit score negatively affected. This would then restrict you on getting approved for more credit in an effort to pay off interest-accruing debt or accessing more money that could increase future returns or cash flow. In the scenario that you are leaving balances on business cards, if you even need to acquire more capital, you can do so since your personal credit score would be unaffected by the high balances on the business side. Business expenses and investing through personal credit cards are for sure doable but ultimately increase risk and could limit you in the scenario where you are not able to pay the debt as planned. Keeping your business spending and investing on the business side ultimately gives you more options and reduces risk. I know people who have invested with money liquidated from personal cards and have found themselves in a bad situation after an investment didn't pay out as expected. This is a scenario you do not want to find yourself in. For these reasons, I strictly use business credit cards for my business expenses or investing.

WHAT YOU CAN DO WITH BUSINESS CREDIT

Maybe at this point, you are thinking exactly how you'd deploy $100K+ into your business or investments you have in mind, but some of you may be asking, "What the heck do I do with $100K+ of 0-percent interest credit" or "What does $100K in credit do for me if I need cash for business or investments?" Well, let's answer those questions right now. First of all, the main reason why businesses fail is due to a lack of working capital. I'm a true believer that if an entrepreneur has access to more money, their chance of success in business increases. With that said, the first option of allocation is if you own a business, fuel your business with more resources to succeed. This might be investing into equipment, an office space, running ads, buying inventory, or paying a mentor to accelerate you on a specific skill. For most businesses, getting through the starting phase is the hardest part, and this is sometimes due to the fact that there are fixed costs. This can be office space, monthly software, staff, or just the initial start-up costs. The sooner you can scale up, the sooner you can increase your profit margins and decrease the percentage of fixed-cost price that is eating away on each sale. For example, in a consulting business, which provides online education, maybe you are paying $1000/month for software and paying an employee $4,000 per month. These are two costs that won't fluctuate much if you had ten customers per month vs. twenty customers per month. So if a little 0-percent business credit can accelerate you to getting to the twenty customers per month in this example, you are able to increase your profit margins and have a high chance of seeing success.

Ok so what if you don't have a business? Well, if you were just approved for $100K of 0-percent interest business credit (like members of Credit Stacking are doing), you now have the ability to start a business or invest the money into something that will make you a great return. Let me list a few examples of what Credit Stacking members have been doing with their 0-percent interest business credit:

- Start a trucking business (or invest into one)
  - Using the credit as a down payment on a truck and letting the month cash flow pay off the truck loan and credit card balance
- Start an Airbnb short-term rental business (or invest into one)
  - Using the credit to pay for rent on properties, which you are then renting out short-term on Airbnb
- Start an e-commerce store
  - Using the credit to launch an e-comm store with a company who runs it for you
- Buy a rental property through the BBBR strategy
  - Using the credit as a down payment and to rehab the property, rent it out, refinance it within the year, and they pay off the credit cards
- Fix-n-Flip a property
  - Using the credit as a down payment on a house that you will rehab and sell within three to twelve months

Additionally, if you are someone who is most interested in seeking more capital to have for things, such as crypto or forex trading, these are also things you can apply your approved 0-percent interest business credit. Now you might be wondering, "How the heck can someone fund crypto or forex from a credit card?" Well, there are secret ways you can liquidate your 0-percent interest credit cards into cash without the crazy high cash advance fees. This is a high-level strategy that is taught inside Credit Stacking, but just know you can turn a $50K 0-percent interest business credit card into cash in as little as twenty-four hours for a very small, single digit fee. This now allows you to spend your $50K on whatever you'd like, which is a major game-changer right here, maybe even read the previous sentence a second time.

BUSINESS CREDIT REQUIREMENTS

Just like anything else that is highly sought after, there are some requirements you should meet before diving into something like 0-percent interest business credit, which I will outline in this section. As we previously went over, your personal credit profile is the foundation that will either set yourself up for success or failure on the business side of credit. And before highlighting them below, I want to remind you again that anything on your credit profile is fixable or malleable. If you don't fit the requirements at the moment, just know that you and everything else can with the right instructions and knowledge. The success that I have had in credit is possible for any entrepreneur as long as you follow the right steps. Some people will be ready today, and for others, it may take a few months to get to, but just know it is possible for everyone to do!

First, you will want to ensure that you do not have any derogatory marks on your personal credit. This means no collections, charge-offs, repossessions, or bankruptcies. Having any of these will have a severe impact on any future credit approvals or size of limits. The only exception in terms of collections is if the collection is a small medical collection. In general, if the collection is from a non-revolving credit account, it's weighted less, but medical collections are weighted the least. The age of the collection and amount will also play a factor in how much it's weighted into your score and any future credit decision. If the collection is aged more than two years, and it's a substantial amount of money, I can sometimes still give my students the go-ahead to proceed, but this is situational based on the rest of their credit profile. And again, if you are someone that is currently set back by derogatory marks, just remember there are ways to get those disputed and removed, which is a crucial first step in most cases before proceeding with credit applications.

Secondly, you will want to make sure you have an incredible payment history. If you remember correctly, payment history is the largest factor of your credit score, which makes up 35 percent of your score. Having late payments can have a very harsh impact on your score, so you will want to make sure you have at least a 99-percent on-time payment history. As late payments age, they will have less of an effect, but they report to your credit report for seven years, so it's important you don't let these happen.

Thirdly, when it comes to the accounts reporting to your credit report, you will see the best results with a variety of accounts to show a solid foundation of personal credit accounts. I have personally seen the best results with at least five primary accounts reporting. The types of accounts will have an effect on your approvals and size of limits, but the more you have, the more trustworthy you look to a lender since it shows you have experience with borrowing money.

Additionally, things like size of limits and age of accounts will have a dramatic effect on your business credit applications. When looking at size limits, you will want to understand the concept of "comparable credit." If you are someone with low limits, it's going to be challenging to get approved for sizable business credit cards approvals. If lenders see that you are responsible with sizable personal credit limits, then they are more inclined to trust you with sizable limits on the business side. For people who need to increase collective limits on the personal side, there are easy ways to, first, increase your limits, and secondly, get approved for high-limit personal cards. Since the average age of these personal accounts have a factor in future business credit card approvals, it's important to prioritize personal credit accounts that offer high limits and also ensure your personal credit score is as high as possible before applying so you will have the highest chance of getting approved for high personal credit card limits. The last thing you will want to do is apply for a variety of personal credit cards and end up with low limits. If the banks see a positive trajectory in limit size over time (your recent approvals being your highest limits), you will see great success on business card limits.

BUSINESS CREDIT CARDS

Anytime you are applying for a new credit card, you will want to make sure it's providing as much value to your business and your life as possible. Each card has different perks and different ways of working for you, and when it comes to choosing the best card for you, it can be a little overwhelming with so many options available to you. When I applied for my first business card, my intention was to apply for a 0-percent business card (Chase Ink Unlimited), but I accidentally filled out an application for a revolving business card (Chase Ink Preferred). Immediately after the approval, I realized how silly of a mistake that was, but in all reality, I was new to the game, wasn't familiar with the certain card benefits, and didn't read the fine print on the benefits. In the long run, the card became extremely useful to me since I started to run ads in my business, but I blew my first shot at getting a 0-percent introductory period on that first initial Chase card, which set me back. This can be common sense to read the details first, but even for a guy like me, I somehow dropped the ball on filling the right application out. But this is a good thing for you because you can learn from my mistakes. To ensure you are getting the right credit cards, it's important to understand the difference between them so you can best maximize the gain you will receive from them.

CREDIT CARD VS. CHARGE CARD

The first type of credit cards I want to outline is the difference between a credit card and a charge card. At first, when I heard the term "charge card," I had no idea how that would be different from a credit card, so please don't feel left out if you don't yet either. The key distinction between the two is that a credit card will allow you to carry a balance and pay it off over time, where a charge card requires you to pay the balance in full.

Each type of credit card is also broken into two categories. *Credit cards* can either be *0-percent interest* cards, which means you have an introductory period on the card, where you can leave a balance and not have to pay any interest on the balance (this can often be twelve to twenty months), whereas *revolving* credit cards allow you to leave a balance, but you are required to pay interest. Technically, both of these types of cards are both *revolving*, but the first subcategory delays the time when interest starts to accrue on the balance, so I like to clarify the difference. Most of the cards you are familiar with are revolving credit cards, such as some of the most common credit cards at Chase, Bank of America, or other top banks. Once the 0-percent interest introductory period expires, the card is now strictly a revolving account, where you have to pay back the balance in full if you don't prefer to pay any interest on the balance.

Not many banks offer *charge cards*, but American Express is the most prominent lender who offers them. The two subcategories of charge cards are *fixed limit* and *no preset spending limit.* When you get approved for a charge card, they are going to give you one of the two types of limits. Fintech banks, such as Capital on Tap and Divvy, are two of the banks that offer fixed limit charge cards, and essentially after running their credit check or reviewing your bank statements, they will give you a set limit you can spend based on their review. Chase Bank just released the Business Ink Premier, which is a fixed limit charge card but can give you more spending power than their traditional credit cards based on your credit file and cash flow. When it comes to the second category of charge cards with *no preset spending limits*, we are going to be looking at the cards offered by American Express. This lender has a large variety of options when it comes to these types of cards. Essentially how this works is they approve you for the card and, based on your spending and payback behavior, they will increase your "spending power" over time. Many people think the limits on these cards are unlimited, which is somewhat true to an extent, but it's something a business owner would need to work toward. When you initially get the card, the "spending power" is going to be relatively low based on your credit score and relationship with American Express, but the more times you are able to max it out and pay it down in full, the more spending power that will give you each month. The first money you could have only $5K in spending power, but the more time you max it out and pay it down, the faster you can get to spending power of, for example, $50K. The analogy I love to give is comparing this type of charge card to a muscle. The more you work out, the larger your muscles get. The more you spend on the card and pay it down, the larger the spending power gets. These types of cards are incredible for a growing business since the spending power can grow simultaneously with the business; however, cash flow is going to be important to pay off the balance accordingly. If you are an e-commerce seller, this could be a perfect type of card for you. Personally, I have four American Express charge cards that have allowed me to massively scale my multiple charge cards, getting my American Express Business Platinum to over $100K in spending power in the first few months.

Here are examples of "no preset spending limit" and "fixed limit" on the bottom of each screenshot:

Aside from making sure you complete the other prerequisites of business credit, you certainly want to make sure you are applying for the cards that provide you and your business with the most positive impact. It will help by asking yourself about what you need the money for and if you need to carry a balance, which will ultimately guide you to making the right choice on your future business credit cards.

Below is a list of some of my favorite business credit cards. I personally have each one, and each has served an incredible purpose in helping me grow my businesses.

- **Chase Bank**
    - Chase Business Ink Unlimited
        - 0% interest for 12 months
    - Chase Business Ink Cash
        - 0% interest for 12 months
    - Chase Business Ink Preferred
        - Revolving card with 3X points on advertising, dining, and travel
- **American Express**
    - Blue Business Cas
        - 0% interest for 12 months
    - Blue Business Plus
        - 0% interest for 12 months
    - Business Platinum
        - Top tier travel charge card
- **US Bank**
    - US Bank Business Platinum
        - 0% interest for 18 months
    - US Bank Business Leverage
        - Revolving card with 2X points on top two categories
- **Bank of America**
    - Bank of America Business Advantage
        - 0% interest for 9 months

FINTECH BUSINESS CARDS

As far as Fintech business cards go, I personally have cards at Divvy, Capital on Tap, and Karat. These kinds of cards are exceptionally helpful since you can get approved for them without a hard inquiry, which leaves your personal score unaffected. Both Divvy and Karat do their underwriting based on your bank statements and use an integration called Plaid that syncs their system to your bank statement so it can read them. The more cash flow and liquidity that is shown through these bank statements, the higher limits you will get approved for. Additionally, there are also ways to increase the size of the approved limit based on the amount of time you need to pay them off. For example, I was approved for $100K on my Divvy card on a monthly statement; however, if I opted to pay it back weekly, they would have increased my limit to $400K! This card is also incredible for the reason that you can get approved for it without a personal guarantee, essentially meaning your business (not you personally) is responsible for paying the debt back. Pretty cool. As far as Capital on Tap goes, as I briefly mentioned, you can get approved for this card with only a soft credit check, no hard pull necessary. These kinds of cards are specifically powerful for businesses that have a fast turnover of cash where the business owner can pay off the balances monthly. For me personally, they have been incredibly helpful for my e-commerce stores, since that is a business that I see a return on monthly and can pay off the balances and keep the cycle repeating.

FUNDING COMPANIES

When it comes to the card applications themselves, there are really two main ways to have them submitted: Do-it-yourself or Done-for-you. The first option (DIY) is what I have been discussing through this entire book and what I believe to be the most effective by far. Something I do want to bring to your attention if you don't already know about them is that there are actually companies that can handle submitting credit card applications for you. Now this might sound convenient; however, there are many negatives that generally come with this experience, which I will clearly outline below. I have personally explored this route for the sake of learning the process and have consulted with dozens of people who have used funding companies, and I'm here to help warn you away from them if you are seeking the most effective route to acquiring 0-percent interest funding for your business or investments.

> **Size of limits:** I'm going to flat out say it, but relying on the strategies a funding company uses on your applications that are submitted compared to the strategies that are taught in this book and in Credit Stacking are unmatched. When it comes to a credit card application, you want to make sure you are maximizing the amount you are approved on each card to prevent opportunity cost. It would make a lot more sense to get approved for a $50K 0-percent interest card than a $25K 0-percent interest card; the only difference is dialing in a few things on your personal credit and applying exactly how I am teaching in this book. If you are missing out on 50 percent of your max funding potential on each card, imagine how that adds up over eight cards. I'm a full sender, and I enjoy maximizing my results to the

fullest, and this is why I prefer the do-it-yourself way. It worked for me and hundreds of other entrepreneurs, producing $50K+ 0-percent interest approvals each week inside of Credit Stacking that the group celebrates.

Amount of hard inquiries: When applying for credit cards, you want to submit them strategically to maximize your effectiveness. It's very rare I get denied for a credit card because I know the exact criteria that each bank is underwriting on and the bureau they will be pulling from. They create more of a "sniper approach," which increases accuracy. This also keeps your hard inquiries low so you can apply for more cards sooner. I like to classify funding companies as the "shotgun approach." No doubt they help get approvals, but relative to the amount of applications they are submitting, it doesn't seem the most effective to me since it leaves some denials behind.

Personal cards: In terms of strategy on applying for credit cards, it's absolutely crucial you don't have too many personal credit accounts opened in the last six and twelve months, as I previously mentioned in this book. Anytime you have too many personal accounts opened in those two time frames, you will be restricted to getting approved for more credit cards. Since there are more personal 0-percent interest cards than 0-percent interest business cards, this makes it very easy for funding companies to opt in on getting their clients approved for their cards to flex better end results on the total amount of 0-percent interest approved for someone. I have previously touched on these points, but I think this is a terrible idea for a few reasons, which I will briefly outline. First, anytime you are leveraging 0-percent interest personal cards, your score will suffer from the high utilization on the balance that you are leaving. Secondly, when it comes to personal credit cards, the non 0-percent interest one often have much better sign-up bonuses, rewards, and benefits, which I think are better to apply for anyway. Thirdly, you cannot remove hard inquiries from open personal credit card accounts, so this restricts you from applying for more cards in the next twelve months. Fourthly, as I mentioned above, if you have too many recently opened personal cards, you are also restricted to applying for more credit card accounts. If you are now using these personal cards for business expenses or investing and now cannot apply for more credit if you need to for the next twelve months, if something unfortunate happens with that business or investment, then you have restricted yourself from borrowing more money from the banks. Ultimately, this will increase the risk of the business spending or investments if you find yourself in this scenario.

Cost of service: Last and not least, funding companies come with a cost. Most funding companies will charge you 10 percent of whatever they help get you approved for. In some scenarios, I have seen fees as high as 15 percent, which, honestly, I just feel bad for people using a service like that and paying such a high fee. Not exactly, but that is just about the same as paying 10–15 percent in interest! Cool, you know you have 0-percent cards, but you are paying a premium to get them. If you are paying 10 percent+ in fees to get them, it will just make your business or investment that much more challenging to be profitable. At the end of the day, I see it as two options: doing it yourself to produce high-limit approvals, or having it done for YouTube to produce average limits, which you have to pay for. I'll choose option one all day.

Last thing I want to mention before I stop ripping into funding companies is the solicitation aspect. I don't know how they are legally able to do this, but it's very common that after you fill out a submission form to a funding company, your phone number somehow gets shared with dozens of other companies that are seeking to get you funding. It's absurd. I literally went through this process myself (and bailed before they submitted any applications for me), and for three straight months, I would receive at least one or two calls from companies trying to pitch me on business funding. I almost changed my phone number because of it, all from this one funding application, and I thought it was a trusted company. Shortly after learning their process and getting bombarded with solicitation, I sooner regretted inquiring in the first place. Well, actually, I don't, because now I get to help other people avoid the same mistakes I made. With all that being said, let me just say this, stay away from funding companies if you want to see better results, save money, and not be solicited for months.

BUSINESS CARD LOCATOR

Searching for 0-percent interest business cards was a more challenging task than I initially imagined when I first got into credit. For some of the top lenders, such as Chase, American Express, and US Bank, finding their 0-percent interest business cards is fairly easy since they are national banks, have very easy websites to locate, and have a great interface that showcases the benefits of the cards. But when you start to narrow your search to national banks that don't have branches in each state, regional banks, or credit unions, it becomes quite challenging and time-consuming to locate the dozens of other cards that are available to you based on your location in the country. I was thinking to myself, *Where the heck is a national database of all banks in the country that offer 0-percent interest business credit cards*, and to my surprise, after hours of research, I could not locate one for the life of me. From that point on, I worked to create this database for myself so I could keep stacking credit. Once I started teaching people about credit, I realized that I would need to make a list of 0-percent interested business cards for each state since this list changes based on where you live. Anyway, over a few months, I was able to complete this database, and I called it the Business Card Locator. The point of it is to reduce the effort someone has to put in to find all of the 0-percent business credit cards in their region. At the moment, this is only available for Credit Stacking members and is a key reason people are able to get approved for so much credit so quickly since the entire list is laid out for them. The last thing I want to do is leave you hanging, so I'll include a preview below of what this resource looks like and briefly touch on how I was able to do the research. I started on Google and YouTube and searched for things like "[Your State] 0% interest business credit cards." The main banks will easily come up and have plenty of information about, so where you have to dive deep is how to find national banks that don't have nationwide branches, regional banks, or credit unions with these types of cards. Once you find some websites to research, you will want to go to their "business" or "Business credit" tab. From here, the keywords you are looking for are "Low Introductory Rate," "0% Intro APR," and "Low Interest." This sounds pretty easy to do, and, really, it's not crazy hard, but for some reason, banks don't prioritize showing the 0-percent interest business card like they are hiding it and don't think people want it more than the other cards. Anyway, you could build your own list of these banks, which offer 0-percent interest business credit cards and start to create your plan of attack this way, which is exactly what I did through my credit journey.

Business Card Locator:

Virginia	Washington	West Virginia
BofA (0%)	Chase (0%)	Chase (0%)
Wells Fargo (0%)	US Bank (0%)	First Community Bank (0%)
BB&T (0%)	BofA (0%)	BB&T (0%)
PNC (0%)	Wells Fargo (0%)	City National Bank
SunTrust (0%)	KeyBank (0%)	United Bank
First Citizens (0%)	Umpqua Bank (0%)	Huntington Bank
Carter Bank & Trust (0%)	Coastal Bank (0%)	Premier Bank
Capital One (0%)	Pacific Premier Bank (0%)	Clear Mountain Bank
Atlantic Union Bank	River View Bank (0%)	
United Bank	Cashmere Valley Bank (0%)	
	Savi Bank (0%)	
	First Federal (0%)	
	Banner Bank	
	WaFd Bank	
	Columbia State Bank	
	Heritage Bank	

INQUIRY STACKING

Stacking your hard inquiries strategically is an art that will allow you to maximize your efforts during each "Credit Stack." As you may know by now, having too many hard inquiries on a bureau prior to a credit card application can restrict you from getting approved. For this reason alone, you want to understand what banks pull from each bureau so you can essentially play Tetris from the hard inquiries you receive from each card. Additionally, each bank weighs inquiries slightly differently, so having the correct order on applications is important; for example, prioritizing a bank like Chase first before American Express because I know that Chase is more strict on the number of hard inquiries in their underwriting process. Another thing that I find interesting and learned over my journey in credit is that banks will pull from a different bureau based on the region you are located in. For example, Bank of America may pull from Transunion if the address on your credit profile is in Washington, but pull from Experian if your personal address is in California. Before submitting any application, I first write out the current inquiries I have on each bureaus and figure out how many I have on each bureau in the last six and twelve months, and then I can figure out which bureaus I can afford hard inquiries on. I then research to see what banks will pull from each bureau based on my region. This information is possible to find yourself, but in Credit Stacking, I provide multiple databases and resources that showcase data points of recent applications in regions across the country to ensure our members have the best insight before submitting their applications. I will include a preview below of what this looks like for data found in Nevada. There you can see that Bank of America and BMO Harris strictly pull from Transunion, where Chase has pulls from both Experian and Equifax. Additionally, some banks pull from only one bureau, some pull from two, and some even pull from three. This allows us to map our six to twelve credit cards to apply for in any given credit stack. Before submitting applications, it's crucial to know what the banks are going to do before executing, so you can maximize your efforts.

Nevada

Bank	Experian Inquiries	Bank	Equifax Inquiries	Bank	Transunion Inquiries
Chase Card	5	Chase Card	3	Exeter FIN	2
Ally Financial	3	CreditPlus	2	CreditPlus	2
USAA Federal Savings Bar	2	CIC Credit	2	CIC Credit	2
Nowcom/Westlake Financi	2	WFDS	1	Barclays Bank DE	2
CIC Credit	2	SouthernCA	1	Bank of America	2
WF Card SVC	1	Rategenius	1	Veridian CU	1
Weststar Credit Union	1	LithiaVW	1	VCU Lending	1
Santander Consumer USA	1	Honda	1	T2 Financial	1
Resident Verify	1	GlobalLend	1	Service FIN	1
Global Lending Service	1	FctualData	1	Lithia VW Au	1
FctualData	1	EMSWellsFB	1	EVILLETEAFCU	1
Equifax	1	EMS	1	Equifax MTG	1
CreditPlus	1	Elements	1	CredCo/CoreLogic	1
Credit Acceptance	1	CredCo/CoreLogic	1	Collins Cred	1
CredCo/CoreLogic	1	Capital One AF	1	COAF	1
Citi Cards CBNA	1	AHFC	1	Citizens One	1
Bank of America	1	WF Card SVC	0	BMO Harris B	1

BUSINESS CREDIT APPLICATIONS

After all the research is done and previously mentioned prerequisites are met, it's now time to execute the plan. This is what it all comes down to, it's crucial you hold the ball tight and make it to the endzone on each application. The two steps below could be a make or break on securing enough 0-percent interest capital to scale your business most effectively or make a new investment.

How to apply: As previously mentioned, the three ways to apply for credit cards consist of online applications, in branch applications, and applications through Business Relationship Managers (RM). Unfortunately, there is so much credit card fraud that happens these days that some online credit card applications can be denied for the sake of something small, such as a flagged VPN, grammar mistake on application, IP address, and so on. If you do online applications, just make sure you give them no reason to think the credit card application is fraudulent. Secondly, you could resort to doing your applications in the branch. This way, they can verify your identity and receive your signature. This ultimately reduced the risk for the bank so it allows for a more favorable decision and limit. Thirdly, and the most effective by far, submitting your applications through a business relationship manager. This is a different person than a regular business banker; these individuals are not the ones who generally hang in the branches and are people who work closely with the underwriting team for these credit decisions. Anytime you are applying for a business credit card through a business relationship manager, it increases the change of the application directly to the underwriting team, which, of course, is better since you now have a human making the credit decisions vs. a computer algorithm like an online application would give you. This is, BY FAR, the best way to apply for business credit cards, no questions asked. The size of your limits are dramatically increased this way. For online or in-branch applications, I have generally seen limit sizes of $15,000–$27,000 on Chase Business Ink cards, for example, but when submitted through a business relationship manager, we generally see limits between $31,000–$75,000, night and day difference. Right now, you might be asking, "How do I find a business relationship manager?" That is a golden question right there. Truthfully, it can be very hard to find one to work with. It took me a long time to figure out how to access these people and convince them to work with me since their line of business is generally for large businesses. With persistence, I was able to build relationships with these individuals across a variety of the top banks that not only help me on all of my business credit card applications but assist Credit Stacking members on theirs. Once someone is ready for the business card applications, I personally make an email introduction, they hop on a quick call, the RM will shoot the application to the applicant, the applicant submits it, and bam. $40,000, $50,000, and $70,000 approvals; like clockwork.

How to fill out the application: At this point, now you know what options you have on submitting applications, but before you hit submit, there are a few things you want to make sure you do correctly. A misstep on the application can easily cause a denial or small limit approval, so this part is almost as important as how to apply. The first thing to be crystal clear on is the accuracy of your information. Your address, DOB, SSN, EIN, full name, business name, and so on needs to be perfectly accurate. If something doesn't match up correctly, there is a very high chance of not getting approved. Before submitting an application, I will thoroughly double check my work and say it out loud to ensure I am not making any mistakes. Next, it will be asking you about your business category or business type. It's incredibly important that this info matches with the info that is on your bank account and syncs with the accurate NAICS code. For example, if your bank account is registered as a trucking company, but you are applying as a consulting company, this may create an unfavorable outcome. Another section you will want to consider are the figures you are reporting for personal income, estimated business revenue, rent/mortgage payment, and if you are employed. The combination of these figures will play a big role in their underwriting. You do not want to report excessively high income or revenue, but I will tell you, it's basically an honor system with the exception of a couple of banks who have asked to verify. For "employment status," if you are an entrepreneur and not technically working a job, I would recommend selecting "employed" (since you are employed by your business) rather than "self-employed." It looks less risky in the eyes of the banks, trust me. Lastly, if you are doing your applications through a relationship manager, there will actually be a text field asking you what limit you are requesting to get approved for (one of the reasons we are able to see those $50K+

limits) and what your estimated monthly spend will be on the card. This is case by case depending on someone's credit profile, bank relationship, and strength of business, but the combination of these two numbers play a major role in the limit size.

We're going to continue to discuss business credit in much more detail when you consider corporate credit in a later chapter. For now, spend your time expanding the businesses you own through the strategies we've covered here. Get that money working for you and keep your accounts clean to avoid rejections. I think you'll find that with the right cards and strategy, the risk you once thought associated with starting and maintaining a business was mostly a myth. I always encourage you to increase your luck and increase your chances of doing well in business by stacking your assets. Credit Stacking is no different. Think of it like a game of cards. You want the deck always stacked in your favor. If you hold the most cards, the likelihood of that being true gets higher and higher. I'm no gambler, but I am a believer in taking calculated risks. I think that the more we make our chances favorable, the more likely we are to benefit from our ventures and the risks we take. Good luck with your credit approval processes!

We'll change up the pace a little bit and get back to some real fundamentals of personal finance in the next chapter.

CHAPTER 5
MONEY

> *With extreme wealth comes extreme responsibility. And the responsibility for me is to invest in creating new businesses, create jobs, employ people, and to put money aside to tackle issues where we can make a difference.*
>
> Richard Branson

After going over business credit and utilizing debt to launch your ideas, we need to stop and take a realistic look at the capital you raise and the profits you generate. What are you going to do with them? In this chapter, we're talking about money. Money can be used to keep your business going and generate even more money for you. And here, we're going to plan out methods to keep that growth and wealth generation going.

This chapter is for you, whether you're building up capital for your business or your own personal needs. The principles work for those building business capital and those building their own capital and developing their own personal assets and wealth. Your goals, life plans, and financial freedom, they're all going to require you to understand wealth and wealth growth to meet the milestones you set for yourself. If you feel there are techniques that work for you here, simply apply them to your unique goals and make sure you apply the same discipline that we've been discussing to that process.

The first principles we need to cover are about wealth accumulation. Starting off, let's go over interest.

PRINCIPLES OF WEALTH

Warren Buffet and Charlie Munger didn't become billionaires in a year or even decade. But over time, compound interest built up and gave them returns upon returns, all contributing to their principle as it expanded, generating even more wealth. Compound interest is simply interest upon interest. For example:

- You start with $100 growing at 10% (an average rate)
    - Your first year, this generates $10 in capital gains, which are reinvested into the account
    - Your second year, your capital gains are now generated for $110 instead of just $100, so your capital gains are $11
    - This keeps going, with the gains themselves increasing as your portfolio increases in principle. By the time you let this compound for 30+ years, the returns get insane relative to the principal invested amount

If you Google "Warren Buffet wealth chart," you'll be able to see the high majority of his wealth was created in the last two decades. Not only does he pick stocks well, but his compounded interest is exceptionally well, which has led him to become one of the richest people in the world. Another thing I'd like you to do is Google "compound interest calculator" and click on the first link. Through this tool, you'll be able to see what future values would look like depending on your initial investment, monthly contribution, length of years compounding for, and the annual interest rate. I constantly find myself using this tool to get myself excited about the wealth I'm seeking to have at a future point in my life. Let me show some examples below through screen shots from the Compound Interest Calculator. In this first example below, you can see that with only a $250,000 initial investment making a 10-percent return (extremely modest return) for forty years, you will end up with over $11,000,000. Isn't that insane?! It makes me wonder how more people do not retire with a net worth of over $10,000,000. Now you might be looking at the $250,000 initial investment and thinking that is exceptionally high. In reality, that is pretty high for most people. But the reality is, with access to money, access to the right investments, and discipline to allocate a good chunk of income to investing, this is possible for anyone to do.

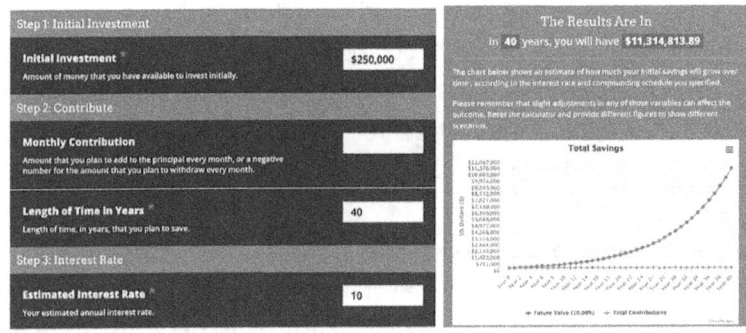

Let's look at an even more exciting example below. In this example, the only changes I made was decreasing the initial investment to $100,000 (much more attainable for most people) and increasing the annual interest rate to 20 percent. This brought the total net worth in forty years to almost $147,000,000!!!

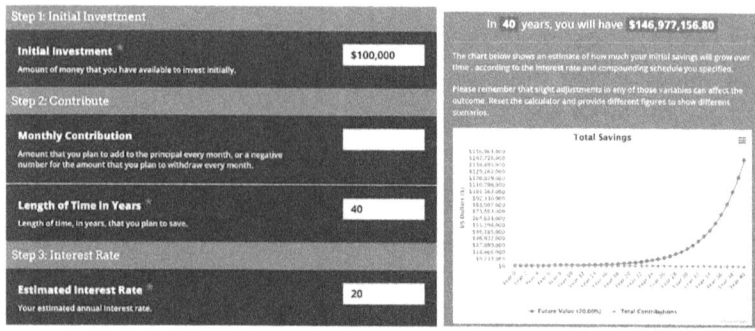

Any average person can put their money into the S&P 500 and make ~10 percent per year (the S&P 500 average over the last ~90 years), so I am personally looking for returns far above the 20-percent mark, if not much, much higher. Many of my investments are actually making greater than 40 percent. Now 40-percent annual returns might not be sustainable for forty years consecutively, but in the scenario where I had a $100K investment compounding for forty years at a 40-percent return, I would have over $70,000,000,000. Again, I am not counting on 40-percent returns for forty straight years, but as you can see, the power of compound interest is a beautiful thing. The sooner you start, the better off you will be!

While there's a lot of information in the world on buying low and selling high, day trading, or predicting markets and timing when you enter and exit, there is a much simpler way to passively approach this system. This is the concept of the dollar cost average.

Dollar cost averaging is the most effective way to invest into something. It's exceptionally hard to time the tops and bottoms of the market, but when you dollar cost average, you are diversifying your risk over time. This has proven through many studies to be, on average, the most effective way to create the best returns, assuming the investment appreciates over an extended period of time. Additionally, this can take out the emotions of investing, which can be very powerful. Anytime someone puts emotion into investing, it can cause more harm than help. An effective dollar cost averaging strategy consists of allocating a specific percentage of your monthly income into your investments. For example, someone could choose a certain percentage, such as 20 percent of their monthly income to invest, whether the market is up, down, and going sideways. If you don't have an investing strategy so far, I would highly consider something like this. Set a specific percentage of your income that you can allocate to investing, and hold yourself to investing it. Again, this strategy has been proven to be the most effective by many studies.

Your returns will expand over time and follow different market trends, but ultimately, there will be a return at the end of the day that should be dramatically higher than inflation, higher than your standard savings account, and of a sufficient amount to return you great capital gains. That is, if you invest that money the right way. This means in a well-diversified portfolio that has down side protection but also incredible growth potential.

I like to keep my stock portfolio simple but diversified. You don't have enough time in a day to keep checking markets and chasing stocks up and down the ticker, but you can invest in a few time-tested companies and a few slightly riskier companies to make a nice combination for growth. When I am making investments into stocks, I am mainly betting on the leader of the organization. For example, in Tesla, I am not only investing in Tesla, but I am also investing in Elon. Looking at the CEO of the company you are investing in, I think, is incredibly important. This is an example of what my brother, father, and I did when we each invested into Tesla in early 2020 around the time when the pandemic hit. Since then, the stock price has over 5Xed at the time of writing this book. I took some profit along the way to lock in some gains and move over to my crypto portfolio (which has also done very well), but my father hasn't sold any of his Tesla shares, which blows my mind when I see the total return he has made. These simple principles we've just covered will set your net worth to skyrocket if you use them patiently. The key is to identify a company with the largest solution in the world who is led by a powerful leader. Investing there and having patience will give someone a good chance of an incredible return. Additionally, one of my father's friends was a relatively early investor in Amazon. I asked him how he was able to identify it so early, and he replied with, "I don't know, it just seemed like Jeff Bezos knew a lot about the internet and was doing it well." In this scenario, my father's friend identified a company providing a big solution to the world with a strong leader and invested into it. It's funny because he sold his shares after they doubled, and it made him $1,000,000 (who can blame him), but after that point, it mooned to incredible new highs. He bought back in along the way, but I thought that was an interesting story to share.

Over time, you'll see your returns compound and your portfolio in a much better place than when you started out. Even with all the success I have enjoyed in business, at my age, I am still way early in the game. It only gets better from here. The best returns on your stocks are yet to come if you're anywhere near where I am in the game. If you're younger, and you are already starting out getting your money into a good portfolio, then get it in there and get it working for you. You have so much time to accumulate those capital gains and benefit from the dividends it produces. The only way to reach financial freedom is through investing. The earlier you start, the faster you will get there. I'm not talking about stock market investing either; investing into anything that will make you a return much higher than the rate of inflation. The December Consumer Price Index (CPI) showed annual inflation hitting 7 percent, which is the highest in thirty-nine years. As I previously mentioned, I'm really only looking for annual returns of greater than 20 percent. You will also need to assess where you are at in your life and determine your risk tolerance. The younger you are, generally the higher risk tolerance you have since you have less to lose and more to gain, as well as more time to recover if something happens. I have a relatively high risk tolerance.

Even if I wiped myself clean through losses, I know I would be able to build it right back again. Would that absolutely suck? Yes, but I do know it's possible based on my knowledge and skill set, which leads me to mention the power of knowledge and having a monetizable skill set, but that's a separate topic. I do set precautions and very cautious investments, but we have one life to live, and I'm trying to make the most of it.

The point I want to make here is that you need to look at your finances and make sure that you are securing your personal finances for yourself and your loved ones. I heard this next line from Grant Cardone, but it's your duty, your obligation, and your responsibility to claim success. No one else is going to do it for you, and it's up to you to claim it. If there is anything that you take from this chapter, take this: The stigma against entrepreneurship that those working for a nine-to-five job may make is that you are only as safe as your job. You might have faced that hesitation when starting off on your own, and you might have thought that you would just be taking all kinds of risks and saying goodbye to financial security. This could not be further from the truth. I have maintained a portfolio to make my money work for me, and my business ventures have only helped accelerate my returns through my investments.

SELF-EDUCATION

When it comes to investments I believe your most powerful investment is you. The more educated, skilled, and connected you are, the more effective you will be for not only generating more active income but also getting access to more lucrative investments and being able to make better decisions on them. The first thing I think anyone should be investing in is self-education. Rather than college, I am specifically talking about investing into online courses and mentorships where you can learn specific skills. I did, in fact, graduate from the University of Washington with a business marketing bachelor's degree, but when I think of the specific skills I use on a daily business to scale my businesses and invest, it's all been through self-education. For me, I received the most value from college from learning discipline of time, speaking in front of groups, and how to operate effectively as a team through group projects. I do think those things are important, but I also think those are skills you can easily acquire through real work or entrepreneurship. I am definitely happy to see online courses and mentorship become more and more popular because I think learning specific skills can be incredibly powerful instead of a generalized education that universities teach. For example, if I am interested in learning how to run ads, I would join a mentorship where I would learn that skill. If I want to learn how to wholesale real estate, I would join a mentorship program where I would learn those strategies. In my scenario, if entrepreneurs want to learn how to get access to hundreds of thousands of dollars of funding for their business or investments, they join my mentorship, Credit Stacking. Through this way of self-education, you are able to expedite your learning through a niche of your choice, which can dramatically increase the speed you see in results and create a gain in your life. Relative to a generalized education of skill set, learning specific skills from experts in a particular field can also decrease the mistakes you make through the process and save you the opportunity cost of learning it slowly by yourself. Additionally, when you are in these mentorship groups you are also joining a community of relatively like-minded individuals who have similar visions or interests. This can make it dramatically more helpful while learning new things if you have support or a community to lean on to help you excel. Joining private groups, for me, which I only started to do in 2019, has been a night and day difference in the rate I am able to learn new things, something I highly recommend to anyone seeking financial freedom. Get yourself out there and into a group that will elevate you!

Leading me to my next point of self-education, I also think it's incredibly important to get yourself in the right networks of people. To piggyback off the above and take it to the next level, if you are trying to learn something specific or enter a new field or industry, you should attend in-person mastermind events. In 2021, this was a new concept for me, but ever since attending such an event, my growth in business and investment has expanded exponentially. Essentially, a mastermind is an event to bring together like-minded people who have often never met before. I've been to mastermind events on credit, tax strategy, investing, passive income, how to scale a business, cryptocurrency, DeFi cryptocurrency, and more. And oftentimes at these events, there will be a handful of speakers who each speak on a different topic.

ROTH IRA

The first financial product I want to discuss in your journey toward financial security is Roth IRA, specifically a self-directed one. This investment tool allows you to invest your money and watch it grow tax-free. This account can be withdrawn after you are 59.5 years old, completely tax-free. You can withdraw earlier but will incur a 10-percent fee if you do and pay tax on it. There is little benefit in withdrawing that early. The point of this account is to grow your money tax-free for years and benefit from the accumulated amount when you reach retirement. This account is contributed along the way at no more than $6,000 a year. I'm highlighting this product because it is so important to get started on accumulating wealth in this account early in your life. It's a product that can help you grow your net worth by investing in the stock market or a select few other funds without significant risk. And if you believe tax rates will be higher later than they are now, this is a great way to hedge against them. When it comes to withdrawal exceptions of your Roth IRA, some of them include $10,000 to go toward your first home purchase, qualified medical expenses, or qualified educational expenses, which are all very helpful. I really enjoy having my Roth IRA because since I can't really touch it until I'm 59.5 years old, it acts as a safety net for me. By knowing I have this account growing for me and is projected to be X amount by the time I'm that age, it gives me more flexibility to be riskier now with my investments that are outside of my Roth IRA. With small contributions, I started mine on Interactive Brokers when I was eighteen and was able to add more and more to it over the years. After additional yearly contributions and some good stock returns since then, I'm happy with the safety net it's going to provide me after it continues to compound for the next ~30 years. Something else that I have done with my Roth IRA account that has accelerated my returns even more is rolling it over into two other types of investments. Remember, you can't actually withdraw the money in the Roth IRA without being penalized, but you do have the ability to transfer it to another "custodian" through a Roth-to-Roth transfer to avoid the penalty and taxation. The first investment I took advantage of was investing into a cryptocurrency hedge fund. Through this unique strategy, I was able to switch the custodian that allowed the money to be invested into such a fund, which enabled me to make tax-free crypto returns. It is pretty incredible that it's even possible to do such a thing, but I'm here to tell you it's possible and doing well. I was able to execute on this strategy when BTC was only priced at ~$13,000 in November 2020, and with that said, it has been the smartest financial decision of my life. The second investment consisted of lending my money to a company that essentially pools up money from "sponsors" (like me in this scenario) and uses it as a bridge loan for high network individuals who are seeking credit approvals on large credit products. I probably would have made better returns if I invested in Tesla through my Interactive Brokers account; however, I'm making over 50-percent APY through this investment, which I still consider phenomenal. Anyway, the point I am trying to make by telling you all of this is that so much is possible through the right knowledge and relationships. Because I learned about a Roth IRA from a young age, I then set up a Roth IRA account, and because I created relationships with people who had good investment ideas who offered a Roth-to-Roth transfer, I was then able to use my Roth IRA account to fund it. I'm super happy you are reading this book because now you are learning about these same strategies. I'm all about empowering others to build lasting wealth, and I think using a Roth IRA can dramatically help. This is possible for anyone reading this book with the right education and action-taking abilities. If you don't already have a Roth IRA investment account, I would research how to set one up on either Interactive Brokers or Charles Schwab.

INFINITE BANKING CONCEPT

There's another idea that I want to help you jump onto as you raise capital through credit stacking. You're going to be experiencing a significant increase in your personal wealth through the tips and tricks in this book, whether you are funding a business or not. Remember, this book is not strictly about raising capital for your business but to accelerate you to financial freedom and help you build lasting wealth.

This next financial tool is something that, if structured properly, can be very effective in accumulating wealth tax-free. It's called the Infinite Banking Concept, and consists of an Indexed Whole Life Insurance policy. There are a variety of incredible benefits to this concept that I will dive into, but one thing to be clear on is that all life insurance policies are not created the same way. And if you are already someone who has heard of this concept or has a life insurance policy already, bear with me to be clear on this exact type. Before getting my policy, I read three books on the topics, watched dozens of YouTube videos, and shopped around to four life insurance agents. Through my extensive research, I'm confident that this type of policy is the best offered on the market.

The specific life insurance policy that I have and am referring to has to be structured in a way where you are maximizing the "cash value" of it, which pushes it as close to an investment in the eyes of the IRS but doesn't trigger something called a MEC. This essentially enables you to pay the absolute least in insurance premiums and gives you the most access to your money to borrow at any future point to use in your life. If the policy is structured with too much cash value, the IRS will consider this as more of an investment rather than a life insurance policy, which would lead you to having to pay tax on it, so the goal is to structure is as aggressive as possible so it doesn't trigger a MEC but maximizing the cash value you have access to in the policy. Essentially, what this financial tool allows you to do is add money into the policy that has already been taxed so that once the money is in the policy, it can grow *tax-free* through the lifetime of the policy. While the money is growing tax-free, the policy also gives you access to your money in the form of a loan. The cool thing about this is the money inside the policy will grow at ~5.5 percent per year. When you take a loan against the policy (against your cash value of the money you have already contributed), you will pay an interest rate of only 5 percent, but the full principal will still be growing at ~5.5 percent per year.

Now you might be thinking that ~5.5 percent might not be that great, but let me dive further so you can understand why this concept is so incredible. Firstly, if you look at a compound interest calculator, ~5.5 percent does, in fact, compound over thirty+ years fairly nicely. Another thing to remember, after the money is in the policy, you do not have to pay tax on this money at any point. This is massive! And this is not like a Roth IRA, where you can't touch your money until your 59.5 years old, you can have access to your money at any point within a matter of a few days. Additionally, there is a special type of policy called an "Indexed Policy," which essentially allows you to ride the returns of the S&P 500. There is both a ceiling and floor to this option, which firstly means you will be capped at about ~12-percent returns (if the S&P 500 increases 15 percent, you will only grow at ~12 percent). As far as the floor goes, the floor is 0 percent. Even if the market and the S&P 500 crashed, you will not face any negative returns (if the S&P 500 decreases 5 percent, you won't face a negative return).

At this point, we have the opportunity to have an investment vehicle that can make up to ~12-percent annual returns, grow tax-free, and give you the ability to borrow against it at only 5 percent while the full principal is growing. Incredible, right?! And I'm not even done with highlighting the benefits.

In addition to the amazing benefits I have outlined so far, there are still two more. The first one is litigation proof. This means no one is able to come after this money; not the courts, an ex-business partner, an ex-wife, NOBODY. This is your money for the rest of your life. And what a peace of mind knowing that no one will be able to touch it. Lastly, you might be wondering what makes this a life insurance policy. Well, it also comes with a death benefit. When you pass away, this death benefit amount will be passed onto your beneficiary. These death benefits are often over $750,000, which can be incredibly helpful to your beneficiary in the scenario of your death. This is literally the last reason why I set up my Indexed Whole Life Insurance policy, but it's a pretty sweet bonus! I am more interested in the tax-free, litigation-proof, cash value returns that I have access to borrow against at any time. The death benefit is just the cherry on top.

At this point, I have talked about taking a loan against your policy quite a few times, so let me dive a little deeper into this topic and do my best to answer any questions:

> **How much of my contributions are split between the premium and cash value portion of the policy?**
> The most aggressive split you can do in a policy like this is 90/10. So 90 percent of your contribution is going toward your cash value (money you have access to and can borrow against) while 10 percent is going toward the insurance premium, which essentially helps cover the $750,000+ death benefits. I mentioned earlier this is the most aggressive way we can push the policy to prevent the IRS from considering this as an investment. To get the tax-free and litigation-proof benefits, it still has to "look" like an insurance policy. An easy way for someone to get ripped off on a life insurance policy is when it's not structured with a similar split. The higher the premium, the fewer benefits for you and the most the insurance broker gets paid.

With the given split outlined above, your cash value generally hits its break-even point at about year five. What this means is it will take you five years to see the exact cash relative to what you contributed. Let me give you an example, if you have a 90/10 policy set up for $20K per year, the first year you will have $18,000 in cash value (90 percent of $20K). In the second year, the same percentage of your contribution will be allocated to cash value, but over the five years, we need to account for the growth of the cash value through its compound interest. So if you were to contribute $20K for ~5 years, you would see your break-even point of having contributed $100K and also having a cash value of $100K. Even though part of your contribution is going toward the death benefit, the compound interest makes up for it. During those first few years, you have to bite the bullet a little bit, but in my opinion, all of the benefits I have outlined in this section highly outweigh the cons.

How much am I able to contribute?
The amount you can contribute is based on the policy structure you set up from the beginning. You would tell the insurance agent how much you'd like to be able to contribute each year, and he would structure it around that amount. For example, if you'd like to contribute $20,000 per year, he would set it up so the premium is $2000 per year (10 percent), and the cash value is $18,000 per year (90 percent). In this scenario, you would not be able to contribute more than $20,000 per year. However, if you skip a year, the contribution limit rolls over to the next year. So if you missed your cash value contribution three years in a row, in the fourth year, you could

contribute $72,000. The only necessary contribution each year is the premium, which, in this scenario, is $2,000. If you had a not-so-fortunate year, you don't have to contribute the full $20,000, but you are still obligated to pay the $2,000 premium. In the scenario you can't pay the premium, you will forgive the benefits moving forward. Additionally, the size of your structure and your results of your health review will determine the size of the death benefit.

How long do I have to contribute?
The length of time you contribute will depend on your preference when setting up the policy, but generally, they are designed to contribute for ten to twenty-five years. After about ten years or so, you wouldn't even need to contribute toward the premium since the interest on your policy would exceed the cost of the premium, so you can have the interest cover the premium payment.

How much can you take a loan for?
You can only take a loan up to the amount of your cash value. So if you contributed $100,000 over five years, your cash value will be around $100,000, which you can borrow this full amount. If your cash value grows and compounds to $900,000 over your life, you can borrow up to $900,000. It is very simple.

What happens if I don't pay the loan back?
If you don't pay the loan back, the only thing that happens is it's deducted dollar for dollar from your death benefit. I see this as practically nothing since I didn't get the policy for the death benefit anyways! In the example that your cash value is $500,000, you

are borrowing the full $500,000, and you die with the $500,000 not paid back; the $500,000 would simply be deducted from your death benefit that is given to your beneficiary. If your death benefit was $900,000, and you were borrowing $500,000 at the time you die, your beneficiary would receive $400,000 instead of the full $900,000.

Where can I learn more on this topic and look at getting a policy?
There are a lot of insurance agents that can write life insurance policies, but most of them don't offer and won't offer such a policy that I have outlined since through this structure, the agent makes less money. I actually used to sell car insurance when I was twenty years old and reached out to my former boss at American Family, and he did not write these kinds of policies. When taking advantage of this financial tool, it's absolutely crucial you find an agent that can set it up with this structure, or you won't be able to take full advantage of it. If you want to dive deeper on learning these topics, I would highly recommend you read the book, *Becoming Your Own Banker*, by Nelson Rash. This was the first of many books I read on this concept, and it blew my mind. In terms of getting access to the same agent who wrote my policy with this exact structure, this is something I do for any member of my Credit Stacking mentorship through a personal introduction by me. If you find yourself in my group at some point in the future, I have extensive videos on this topic and a recorded interview with my agent that outlines this concept in more detail. But at this point, you know exactly what

to look for and how to make sure you don't end up getting a life insurance policy with subpar benefits.

CRYPTOCURRENCY

Another point I want to touch on in this chapter is cryptocurrency, something that I am heavily invested in and think will change how the world will operate financially. Now I know this book is primarily focused on building credit and getting access, but after someone gets access to money and has a better advantage to make money, I think it's incredibly important that they are educated about ways they can invest their money. Through investing your money is working for you, and not the other way around.

We've all heard so much about cryptos in the last few years, and depending on where you stand, you either think it's going to end the world or save it. I find myself on the right side, seeing it as a product to help return great gains over both the short and long-term and ultimately providing a hedge against the inflating dollar. There are thousands of cryptocurrencies, but Bitcoin is the first ever created crypto, which was founded by the mysterious and unknown character of Satoshi Nakamoto in 2008. It's currently the largest by market capitalization at ~$850B (total money invested into Bitcoin).

"Bitcoin uses peer-to-peer technology to operate with no central authority or banks; managing transactions and the issuing of bitcoins is carried out collectively by the network. Bitcoin is open-source; its design is public, nobody owns or controls Bitcoin and everyone can take part."–Bitcoin.org

Bitcoin isn't necessarily considered to be a currency used to pay people due to inefficiencies in speed; however, it acts as a store of value. Relatively similar to gold, Bitcoin has a fixed supply. There will only ever be 21 million Bitcoins in the world, and at the time I am writing this book, about 19 million have already been mined. It's truly the only type of currency that is fixed. Even when we look at gold, there are small amounts of gold that are miners, and who knows, maybe small meteorites will continue to hit the earth and supply us with more gold. One thing we do know for certain is that there will only ever be 21 million bitcoins. When we compare this type of currency to the US dollar or any other "fiat" currency (a government-issued currency that is not backed by a commodity, such as gold), it's extremely powerful in the sense that it's deflationary. While the US dollar goes down each year through inflation, Bitcoin is likely to increase in value over time due to its fixed supply.

What's crazy is that the market cap of gold is $11.5T, but the properties of Bitcoin are better in every way. It has a finite supply, it's digital, and it's easy to transfer to others. With simple math, if the market cap of Bitcoin reached the same market cap of gold, it would put the price per Bitcoin at ~$500K. I personally do not have a reason to believe that will not happen in my lifetime. To add more context of how small I think the market cap of Bitcoin is, Tesla alone has a market cap that's larger.

The second largest crypto currency is Ethereum (ETH), at a current market cap of ~$425B. What many people don't understand about Ethereum is the fact that it's built on its own blockchain that allows other projects to be built on top of its blockchain. Where Bitcoin is considered as digital gold, Ethereum is considered as "programmable money," which offers much more functionality than Bitcoin does.

In 2021, El Salvador became the first nation to make Bitcoin a legal tender for its country. As of January 2022, its president, Nayib Bukele, has purchased 1,370 Bitcoins with government money. At the current price of Bitcoin (~$40K), this is about a value of $60M. Additionally, cities such as Rio De Janeiro and Miami are also invested in crypto. Rio De Janeiro officially stated they intend to invest 1 percent of their treasury reserves into Bitcoin, and Miami created its own cryptocurrency, named MiamiCoin.

With all that said, I'm incredibly bullish on BTC, ETH, and a variety of other crypto projects that I believe will enhance the lives of humans. Cryptocurrency is the new "internet." Similar to Jeff Bezos, people who knew the most about the internet in the late 1990s generally became the most wealthy through the following two decades. Right now, I see it as the people who are the most knowledgeable and invested in crypto will generate the most wealth in the next few decades. Anyone else who neglects learning or investing into cryptocurrency I believe will have a much harder time keeping up or will simply get left behind. Crypto is here to stay and is here to help elevate humanity.

There are many ways to get involved in crypto, but let's go over my strategy of where I buy and hold my crypto. There are three types of places where I hold my crypto investments, each for a very specific benefit that have helped diversify my portfolio and expedite returns.

CENTRALIZED EXCHANGES:

The category of place where I hold my crypto is on central exchanges, which are exchanges held by private or publicly traded companies that offer investors a platform to trade on. This consists of major platforms, such as Coinbase Pro, Binance, Crypto.com, Voyager, Nexo, Celsius, and KuCoin. Even Robinhood and other stock trading apps who offer buying and selling of Bitcoin is an example of a centralized exchange, but for this type, I will highlight my three favorite below:

> *Voyager:* Voyager, in my opinion, has the best user interface. It's incredibly easy to buy and sell, see your returns on different lengths of time, offers a large variety of tokens to buy, and also shows you

the collection net gain or loss you have made on your account, which is very helpful and not something that other centralized exchanges do at the moment. Voyager is only a mobile app, so it's only accessible from a phone, which has its negatives there, but the app is very clean and easy, so that is no problem for me. Additionally, you can deposit and withdraw USD to and from your bank account very easily, so no fee. This is also an interest-bearing account, which pays very APY on most of the tokens you hold in your Voyager wallet. For example, they pay out 9-percent APY on USDC, 6.25-percent APY on BTC, 8-percent APY on DOT, as well as slightly less APY on most other tokens available on Voyager. For any of the tokens I am holding that pay interest on Voyager, I hold them here.

Nexo.io: Nexo is another centralized exchange that is quite popular and offers a specific feature that I find incredibly helpful. This consists of a lending tool that allows you to borrow against the crypto in your Nexo wallet as collateral. For top cryptos, such as BTC and ETH, you can borrow 50-percent loan-to-value (LTV). If you have $50K in BTC on Nexo, you have the ability to borrow 25 percent of it at any given time. With the exception of USDC at 90-percent LTV, most other tokens on Nexo you can borrow at 33-percent LTV. When it comes to your determined interest rates on the loan, they start at 13.9 percent and can be decreased down to 6.9 percent if you are able to have at least 10 percent of your portfolio balance in NEXO token. Additionally, Nexo pays interest on the token you hold on the platform, which helps offset the interest you are paying on a loan. All in all, I really enjoy being able to borrow money against part of the crypto portfolio through this platform.

KuCoin: KuCoin is the third centralized exchange that I use. The main reason I use this exchange is for the variety of tokens that I am able to buy on its platform. It's a less popular exchange than Nexo or Voyager, but it does have a larger list of tokens to choose from, especially tokens that are outside the top fifty list in terms of market cap. For example, tokens like KDA and ONE are not available on Voyager and Nexo but are available on KuCoin. There is both a mobile and desktop version, which each has a great interface and good user experience. There are also really good safety measures like requiring a trading password to make trades and two-factor-authentication through the Google Authenticator app and through email or text that makes the platform very secure. On KuCoin, you also have the option to buy 3X leveraged tokens to increase your gains on top projects, such as Luna, Polkadot, Cosmos, and more. There is a small management fee on these types of tokens, but for relatively short holds, that can be extremely lucrative if the market is pumping, which essentially multiplies your returns by three. If you'd like to get a 3X leverage long token on Cosmos, you can find it on KuCoin as ATOM3L. But be careful if you buy it since your returns will be multiplied by three, whichever direction it goes.

CRYPTO HEDGE FUND:

As I briefly mentioned above in the Roth IRA section, I am also invested in a cryptocurrency hedge fund. Within the fund, the fund managers are responsible for all of the trades and delivering attractive results to their limited partners, such as myself. Since I joined the fund in November 2020 as investor #8, the fund had produced me over a 5X return at its highest point, which had outperformed the appreciation of Bitcoin after their fees were deducted. In the fund, I actually created two accounts, one for my Roth IRA account (which is money I can't really touch until I'm 59.5) and a second one under one of my business entities. In addition to the performance that it's experienced, one of the main reasons I enjoy this investment is knowing that it's managed by professionals who are trading solely based on the data, with as little emotion as possible. They are constantly optimizing the allocation of cryptos in the fund, locking in profits as the market rises, and rebuying when the market corrects. Because of their full-time research of fundamentals, technicals, and on-chain data (information regarding all transactions that occur on the blockchain network), they have a better idea about what the market is going to do better than anyone I know. At the moment, the minimum to join the fund is $100K, but if you are someone that is interested to learn more and has $100K liquid, you can shoot me a DM on Instagram referencing the crypto hedge fund, and I can send you more information.

DECENTRALIZED FINANCE CRYPTOCURRENCY (DEFI)

The third category of where I hold my crypto leads me into the next section of decentralized finance cryptocurrency, also known as DeFi. This is such a powerful topic there could be an entire book written about it, but I'll do my best to summarize it in this section below. This has been a short break from all the strategies for credit accumulation, but I think it's important to emphasize that my reason for writing this book is to do everything in my power to help entrepreneurs accelerate financial freedom. As I have mentioned a variety of times already, getting access to money is the first step. Once you have access to money or are now making money through active income, it's time to allocate money into ways that make passive income. Over the last two years, I have seen the most lucrative ways to make passive income through e-commerce stores and DeFi crypto. The returns of DeFi are the best I have ever seen in my life.

So, what exactly is DeFi? Well, decentralized finance removes the intermediary (i.e., the bank and institutions between you and financial freedom. By getting involved in DeFi, you will start to become your own bank. How does it work? First you will want to enter the market safely with the proper security measures put into place. This would consist of buying a trusted hard wallet for your crypto, downloading antivirus software, purchasing a VPN, creating a crypto specific email, and so on. These are all precautions that will protect your crypto from any hackers or people trying to steal it. By moving your crypto from centralized exchanges to hard wallets, you are actually taking control of your crypto. When you are "owning" Bitcoin on centralized exchanges, you don't actually own real Bitcoin. The centralized exchange owns the Bitcoin, and they just give you a balance of whatever amount you purchased. When you send your Bitcoin to a DeFi exchange, the true ownership goes to you. Your Bitcoin is digitally stored on the blockchain and will be accessible through your hard wallet, such as a Ledger Nano X, which is the crypto hard wallet that I have. To set up your hard wallet, you will be assigned a twenty-one-word seed phrase and choose a pin code that you will use to access your wallet, where you can then move or swap your cryptos. Every time your crypto is moved or swapped through your hard wallet, you will actually have to confirm the contractions by entering in your wallet pin, which signs the smart contract on the blockchain that allows it to move or be swapped for another token or staked into a yield farm or liquidity pool. But we will get into that in a bit.

Something that I have learned from my DeFi mentor, Gven Sariol, is when determining your allocation of crypto, you will want to allocate at all times 25 percent of your portfolio to stable coins. Stable coins are pegged to the US dollar, so they don't have appreciation or depreciation aside from what the US dollar naturally depreciates. It's like holding digital cash but better! Better because you have the ability to actually make real interest on your stable coins. Well, how do you do that exactly? Let me provide some context to explain why you are able to make 20-percent+ APY on your stable coins. If you look at things like the NASDAQ, New York Stock Exchange, or Coinbase, they are all making billions of dollars through the transaction fees that people are paying to trade. When you look at exchanges like these, they are the ones who are providing the liquidity that facilitates people to trade. For example, if I was buying a share of Tesla at the same time you were selling it on the NASDAQ, you wouldn't be selling it directly to me, you'd be selling it to the NASDAQ exchange, which I would then buy from the exchange. For them to do that, the NASDAQ needs enough money (liquidity) to buy it from you before selling it to me. They are supplying the liquidity that is facilitating the trade, which is why they are able to charge transaction fees. In DeFi, it's very similar. When members of the community are supplying liquidity to liquidity pools (also called "yield farms"), they are providing liquidity for other people to trade between those two pairs, and in return for supplying the liquidity, they are rewarded through APY. This APY is generated through the transaction fees that people are paying to trade between a pair of tokens (whichever token pair they are providing liquidity in). For example, if we look at the liquidity pool FRAX/USDC, right now I am making over 30-percent APY. In this example, for anyone that is trading FRAX to USDC or the other way (both are stable coins, by the way), they are paying a transaction fee, which is ultimately broken up and paid to each person who is providing liquidity to the FRAX/USDC pair. The return for the S&P 500 over 2020 was ~18 percent (which was one of its better years), and here we are making 30-percent+ holding a crypto that is pegged to the exact value of a dollar. Lower risk and higher returns—now that's what I'm talking about!

Since the tokens in the above example yield farm were both stable coins, this creates the lowest amount of risk. For the remaining 75 percent of my DeFi portfolio, I'm investing into higher yield farms that are associated with more risk. You can do this by supplying liquidity to farms/pools, where only one of the two tokens in the pair are stable coins, or even choose farms/pools that don't include a stable coin. These types are certainly riskier but can yield incredibly higher returns. I am currently in a farm that is making me over 250-percent APY, and one of the tokens in the pair is a stable coin; moderate risk, exceptionally high returns.

Another thing that's incredibly powerful in DeFi is the ability to borrow against your crypto. There are a variety of DeFi lending platforms that allow you to take loans with your crypto being the collateral. No credit checks, no applications, no asking for permission, none of that! It's your money and ability to take a loan out immediately at your discretion. You are now your own bank! Also, since loans are not taxable, you won't be taxed on the loaned money and now have additional working capital to increase your investments. What's even more cool is that your principal will be earning single digit interest, which, in some cases, makes your loan almost free to take out. Some of these DeFi lending platforms consist of Venus and AAVE.

The truth is, crypto, in general, can be incredibly risky. But if you are well educated and get involved with the right strategies and precautions in places, there are absolutely incredible gains to take advantage of, literally the best returns I have ever seen or experienced firsthand. I was fortunate enough to be mentored by Gven Sariol (or "Swami Crypto"), who is now a good friend of mine. When COVID crashed the market in March 2020, he had just $15K to his name. At this point, he went all in on DeFi crypto and was able to make over $1,000,000 through the same strategies he's taught me. He now has a mentorship program, where he is teaching hundreds of hungry investors who are seeking financial freedom as well. When explaining DeFi above, I tried my best to give you enough detail to emphasize its power. Since the topic of DeFi is incredibly big, and very in-depth, I tried hard to not overload you with too much info. However, if you are interested in learning about DeFi on a high level so you can make 100-percent APY returns and become your own bank, then I highly encourage you to DM me "DeFi" on Instagram so I can send you information that will help enable this for you. I see the biggest investing opportunity over the next decade being in crypto and DeFi and plan to focus much more of my time and financial resources toward it. It certainly takes time to learn it and implement the strategies, but it's incredibly rewarding. If you want to join me on the journey, shoot me a message so I can let you know you can.

Growing your wealth is a process that is intensely satisfying to watch over time. As you are able to get access to money through credit to help you increase your active income, in my opinion, it's incredibly important to make sure your income is then allocated into places that will multiply it. Over time, it becomes incredibly fun to watch your net worth grow, knowing that you will be taking care of your future self and family. If you don't know where to start with investing and are interested to take what I have been talking about to the next level, I highly encourage you to head to CreditStacking.com and book a free strategy session to learn about what's covered in our program, not only how to get access to $100K+ of 0-percent interest business credit but access to investment opportunities that are proven to make me money and are shareable to my group. I also go into more details on the power of each of these investments or ways to grow or protect your wealth. Anyway, I hope you received great value from this chapter. Each topic has changed my life in an incredible way, and I certainly hope you are able to take advantage as well. I'm really excited for this next chapter. After we get access to money and invest our money to make a passive return, it's time to show you the amazing places that credit allows you to go and enjoy.

CHAPTER 6
TRAVELING ON CREDIT

Travel is never a matter of money, but of courage.

Paulo Coelho

When I started out my journey as an entrepreneur, I never wanted to remain static somewhere and only stick to my business. My love for all things travel has been a key component of my life, from my time as a snowboarder to the travel business my brother and I built in Cabo and to the online business that I am currently running. This love of travel really started with my dad, who treated time with his family as being more important to him than being stuck to his desk nine to five and working all the time. Seeing how he was able to balance his work life with his personal life has really stayed with me in designing my own life and goals. I've now been traveling full time for over a year and cannot recommend the flexibility enough to people I meet and coach. I mentioned my dad before, and once again, this section of the book brings me right back to the things I learned from him. From a young age, I learned the importance of travel. Watching my dad's business managed in a way that allowed him time to travel with us made that nine-to-five grind nothing like the life I wanted to live.

People were made to travel; we've been doing it since the beginning of time. As the methods of travel have become more efficient, we're more likely to go places and see things that our ancestors never dreamed of. The twenty-first century has given us the opportunity to run businesses online like e-commerce, affiliate marketing, influencing, consulting, and many other forms of remote income that can give you the chance to explore the world while reaching your goals for yourself and your business. It's no surprise to me that the founder of Amazon said that the concept of work-life balance is debilitating to the individual. He prefers to refer to it as "work-life harmony," where the two work together to give you the kind of life you want to live.

Bezos is noted for saying "This work-life harmony thing is what I try to teach young employees and actually senior executives at Amazon too."

The importance of this harmony between your work and, really, your life cannot be overemphasized. You don't want to succeed at your business but lose your family, freedom, or the things you enjoy in life. Nothing is worth that price. I've met many people who have told me that travel was something they did not have much time for and that the expenses made it impractical for them. Unfortunately, that is mostly something that people have come to believe because they don't know how to open up opportunities for travel. However, you're going to learn them here. It's not always easy, while starting a business, to focus on a leisure activity, such as travel, but traveling can open up your mind like nothing else, leaving you more inspired and creative than ever. At least that is what it did for me.

At the current age of twenty-eight, I have been to more countries than the number of years I have lived. With the exception of having an apartment in Miami for six months (which I was rarely staying at), I've been traveling full time for almost two and a half years now. After I ended a sales job I was working in 2019, my brother and I packed a suitcase and moved to Bali, Indonesia, where we lived for a total of three months. In Bali, we started an Airbnb rental arbitrage business, which actually got smoked by COVID a few months later, but that only led me onto bigger and better things. Anyway, while building a seven-figure e-commerce business and multiple six-figure consulting businesses, I have been traveling full time. The strategy that allowed me to do this would generally consists of spending one to eight weeks in each location. I did this on Oahu, Gold Canyon (AZ), Cabo San Lucas (multiple times), Washington, Georgia, Tulum, Mykonos, San Diego, Los Angeles, and Miami. Now this might sound hard to manage and expensive to many, but I have been doing it for so long that I have learned the most effective and cost-efficient way to do it, which I will be outlining in the chapter.

One thing I will add here is that to ensure your business is operating effectively and you are staying in good health, finding accommodations with good Wi-Fi and access to fitness is crucial. Slow and unreliable Wi-Fi will certainly not cut it. For fitness, a gym isn't already crucial, but access to an ocean for swims or nice walking trails can be very effective to ensure you are staying in great shape.

In this chapter, I want to show you that traveling and creating financial success does not have to come at the expense of the other. I will be going over the many benefits that credit stacking and just travel education alone can unlock for you in the world of travel. The travel benefits that naturally come within the credit game are quite incredible if utilized properly, but I'm also going to dive into strategies that you can use without credit that will transform the way you think about the expense behind traveling.

Some of the things I'm going to highlight in the chapter consist of credit card point accumulation strategies, credit card point redemption strategies, travel benefits that are included with top travel cards, ways to gain status at airlines and hotels, with and without credit, and secret travel industry passes. Each brings a large amount of value to the table in terms of providing you with an incredible travel experience for great value. Sometimes I will compare these travel hacking strategies to tax strategies. The only difference is knowledge. Anyone can reduce their tax liability if you know the right tax strategies, and the same thing goes for travel. No destination should be too expensive for someone. There is always a workaround and a way to dramatically reduce the cost of it by leveraging the benefits that come with credit and other travel hacking tips.

Before we dive into all things credit points-related, I want to provide some context on what these are and how to value them. Afterward, I'll jump into how to accumulate and redeem them effectively for things, such as free travel. Credit card points are ways for banks to incentivize its users to not only sign up for the card but also to spend on the card. Once you have credit points, you are able to redeem them for things, such as cash back, gift cards, and travel. There are ways to redeem them for excellent value, and there are ways to redeem them for very low value, so it's important you read closely through this chapter so you can ensure you are getting the most bang for your points.

The first category of points are the points you can have with big banks, such as Chase, American Express, US Bank, Capital One, Citi, Bank of America, and Wells Fargo. These points typically hold the most value and allow you to get more value from each point compared to other reward programs. Some banks allow you to transfer the points to partners, while others don't. For example, Chase and American Express allow you to transfer your points to other reward programs, such as hotels or airline companies. This alone makes the points at these two banks more valuable than banks that do not allow you to transfer the points out like US Bank. The other category of points are with the airline or hotel reward programs directly, such as Hilton, Hyatt, Marriott, American Airlines, and each of the other airline reward programs. Even though essentially the same thing, rewards with banks or hotels are referred to as "points," whereas rewards with airlines are referred to as "miles." Once points are transferred from a bank to a hotel or airline platform, they really only have one value, and that is to book travel on their respective travel portals. For example, if you have Marriott points, you can only book Marriott hotels. If you have United points, you can only book flights through the United Airlines portal (United and United airline partner flights). Not all points are valued the same, essentially meaning that some reward programs will allow you to get more monetary value with the same number of points as other reward programs. Chase and American Express points are valued the highest and are the most sought after. Points are valued anywhere between 0.6–2 cents, depending on the program. At a 1 cent per point valuation, 100,000 points are worth $1,000. When you have credit card and reward points and the right strategy on redeeming them, you are able to 5X+ the value of these points, making luxury travel much more attainable for the average person on a sub six-figure salary. In the previous example, this would increase the $1,000 value of 100,000 points to the value of $5,000.

CREDIT CARD POINTS ACCUMULATION STRATEGIES

To take full advantage of credit card points, the first step is to accumulate them. Under this section, I'm going to break it up into three subcategories that will help you rapidly accumulate points. The first effective strategy to take advantage of is through "sign-up bonus" offers. Most banks will offer bonuses on their credit cards to incentivize users to apply for them, which can come in the form of straight cash back or through gifting its users credit card points or miles. On the low end, this can start only around 20,000 points but can range as high as 180,000 points. Through this strategy, we are obviously going to prioritize the cards that offer the largest incentives so we can maximize them through redemption at a later point. Some cards will require a certain spend minimum to earn the sign up bonus, where some cards will give them to you with only an initial small purchase.

Generally, you can expect to have to spend a few thousand dollars on the card in the first three to six months. When getting a card, it's very important you plan accordingly to be able to spend enough to hit the sign-up bonus. I would never recommend spending above your means to hit these bonuses, but you definitely want to be strategic to make sure you meet them if you plan to apply for the card. For example, if you see a card with a 100,000 sign-up bonus and notice that the spending minimum is $10,000 within the first months of having the card, I would recommend to forecast your estimated expenses, and if you think you'd be able to naturally spend that much in that time period, then it would probably be a good idea to attempt. If you need to wait a few months before you plan on doing much spending, that's fine as well. But in the scenario you apply for the card and don't meet the minimum spend, you will not get the sign-up bonus, which would be a bit of wasted effort. So please plan accordingly to ensure you will meet the spend minimum so you can lock in the points through this strategy.

Below are some examples of credit card offers with sign-up bonuses above 100,000 points:

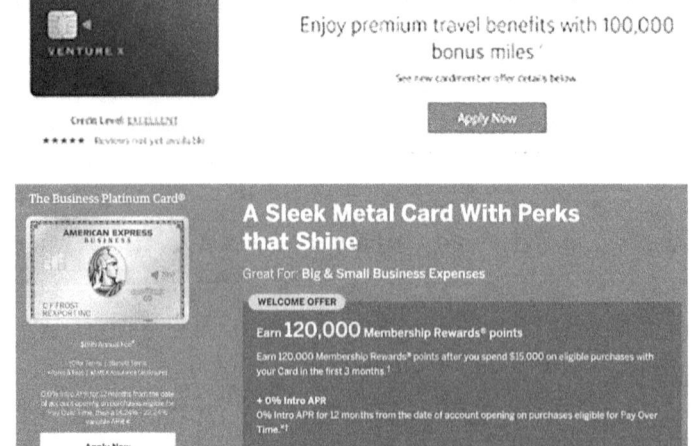

Hilton Honors American Express® Surpass® Card

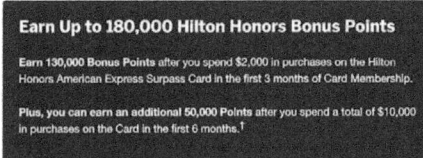

Earn Up to 180,000 Hilton Honors Bonus Points

Earn 130,000 Bonus Points after you spend $2,000 in purchases on the Hilton Honors American Express Surpass Card in the first 3 months of Card Membership.

Plus, you can earn an additional 50,000 Points after you spend a total of $10,000 in purchases on the Card in the first 6 months.†

Earn 100,000 Bonus Points

INK BUSINESS PREFERRED®

Apply Now

***Offer Details | ††Pricing & Terms

$95 ANNUAL FEE†††

After you spend $15,000 on purchases in the first 3 months after account opening***

As you can see, accumulating points through sign-up bonuses can add up pretty quickly. One thing to also know about sign-up bonuses is that some banks will allow you to receive the sign-up offer each time you get approved for the card, but American Express, for example, has a "one-in-a-lifetime" rule that restricts you from getting the sign-up bonus on the same card type twice in your life. This makes it even more important that you are able to meet that minimum spend on American Express sign-up offers after you get approved so you don't miss out on your one shot of getting the bonus on that certain credit card product.

For the second subcategory of credit card point accumulation strategies, I am going to focus on gain points through credit card affiliate links. Just like with most online referral-based financial products, such as bank accounts, stock trading accounts, or crypto exchanges, banks will award its credit card user with additional incentives when they refer people to start using their products. Each bank and credit card will have its own structure on how they incentivize its users to refer people, but, generally, this can award you with 20,000 points per person who gets approved for a certain credit card if they applied for the credit card through your affiliate link. Most cards will have a yearly limit on how many points you can accumulate through your affiliate links, but this generally can range between 55K–100K points per card in any given calendar year. I assume you have friends or people you know who will be applying for credit cards in the near future, and they might as well use your affiliate links! Not only do you get a kickback, but they would also be getting a nice sign-up bonus for applying through your link, a win-win! Say, for example, you were approved for three of the above credit cards, which have each awarded you with 100,000+ in points through sign-up bonuses in addition to referring five friends to each card. After receiving ~20,000 per referred friend, you'd receive an extra 300,000 points just through your affiliate links! If you add this to the 300,000 points you received through the sign-up bonuses, that is a total of 600,000. At a 1 cent to 1 point ratio, that's a value of $6,000! However, once you take advantage of the strategies I'm about to teach you later in this chapter, you'll see how you can 3-5X the value of those points, which would bring you to $18,000–$30,000 in free travel! It's absolutely crazy what you can do with credit in terms of travel with the right information and strategies. It just blows my mind even writing it out for you like this. If you take a look at my Instagram page (@kingofdebt), you can see examples of the travel I have been doing around the world leveraging credit card points. I'm a super frugal guy and prefer to allocate my money to investment instead of blowing it on unnecessary things, but I see credit card points as such an easy ticket to travel the world in luxury.

When it comes to finding your referral links, you can locate them in your bank's apps under a section called "refer-a-friend." Below are a few examples of the referral bonuses you'd receive on a few cards as well as the yearly limit they cap you at. Please don't sleep on credit card referrals, though. It's an incredible way to accumulate points that can lead to an insane amount of free travel.

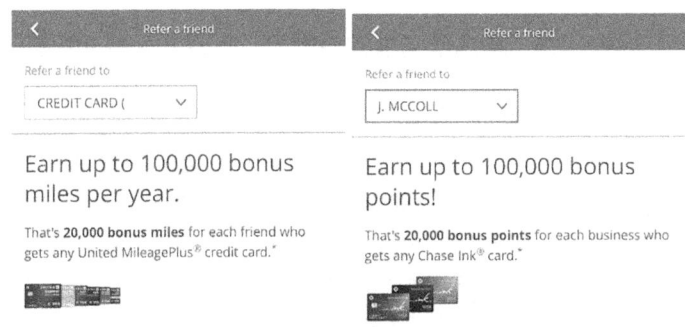

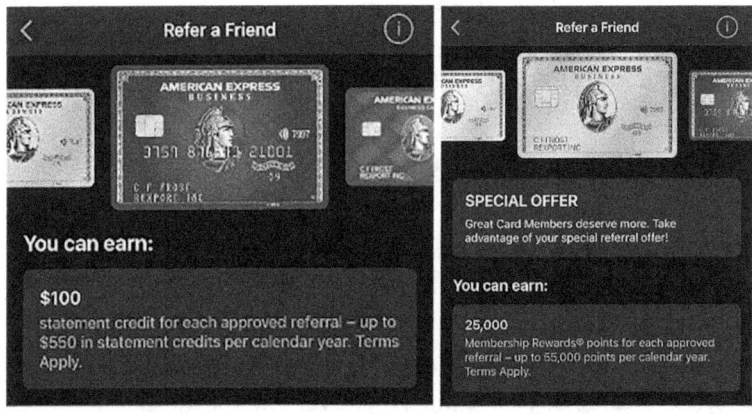

Moving to the third subcategory, I want to dive into strategic spending. As you know by now, each card has an incentive for different types of spending based on the category of transaction. Some cards give higher incentives to spend on travel, where other cards give higher incentives to spend on things, such as advertising, gas stations, or office supplies. Before any purchase I am making, I am always asking myself, "What category of spending will this be considered as?" Based on the category, I will use the appropriate card that I have, which gives the best rewards. For travel and dining I will always use my Chase Sapphire Reserve (3X points per dollar), for advertising, I will use my Amex Business Gold (4X), for gas stations, I will use my Chase Freedom Unlimited (1.5X), and so on. This definitely takes a little thought before swiping your card but highly pays off when being strategic. Organically, I'll be able to generate hundreds of thousands of points per year. And if you are someone who runs ads for your business, if you are spending $10K a month, you will be able to earn 40K points per month if using the right card. If you spend $3K on travel expenses per month, you'd easily be able to earn 9K points per month. This can add up very quickly! Something that I have seen people do to remind them of what card to use is to place a piece of tape on the credit card and write down the best use for that specific card. For example, on the Chase Freedom Unlimited you could write "gas and most daily expenses."

CREDIT CARD POINTS REDEMPTION STRATEGIES

Before we start redeeming any of our points that we worked so strategically to accumulate, it's crucial that you have a good strategy on redeeming them if you are interested in maximizing their value. You might be the same way, but if I have the option to multiply the value of something, then I'm certainly going to do it. Any person can get an average redemption value on points, but it takes a little skill to be able to 3X+ the value of your points. If you remember the example above through accumulating 600K points through sign-up bonuses and affiliate bonuses, if used strategically, you would be able to increase the 1:1 value of $6K to 3:1 value to $18K (if not higher). I have funded much of my luxury travel from the redemption strategies I'm about to go over. This chapter is all about making sure you have the knowledge to get the most bang per point. Many people who are stuck in a sub six-figure salary think that extravagant vacations are out of reach, but I am here to tell you that through the strategies I am about to teach out, that luxury travel to iconic global destination is certainly within reach for very little if any money at all (in terms of flights and accommodations).

Not only are there different rates for accumulation as I previously went over, but there are also different places and products involved in the redemption process that net higher rates of return. Before we dive into how to maximize your points, I first want to clarify the ways you can redeem your points that I advocate against. We will primarily first at Chase and American Express points and the options you have in spending your point through each of their travel portals.

When you log in to each portal, you will see a variety of options each bank presents to you on ways you can spend your points. You will see cash back, statement credits, gift cards, options to buy merchandise directly from certain merchants, or through booking travel directly through their travel portal. For the average person, these all can look like decent options. Generally, my rule of thumb is you are getting a bad redemption value on points if you are getting a 1:1 ratio or less, a fair decent redemption value on point if you are getting above 1:1 ratio, a good redemption value on points if you are a 1.5:1 or higher, and an excellent redemption value on points if you are getting a 3:1 ratio or better. We are in the game of looking to at least 3X our points here!

Let's chunk them down and clarify the value you'd receive from each.

- Redeeming points on Amazon or through PayPal
  - Only gives you 0.8:1 value on your points (20% less than 1:1 value).
- Redeeming points for Apply merchandise
  - Only gives you 1:1 value on your points
- Redeeming points for gift cards
  - Only gives you 0.9–1:1 value on you points
- Redeeming points for cashback
  - Only gives you 1:1 value on your points

(Example of redeeming points for gift cards at a 0.9–1:1 ratio)

CREDIT STACKING

(Example of redeeming points for cash back at a 1:1 ratio)

With the options above outlined, I would strongly advise any of them if you are someone who likes to get the most value out of things. Like I said, anything equal to 1:1 or less is, in my opinion, a bad redemption on your points. Now let's move to a few options that will give you above a 1:1 value.

First, I would like to highlight that there are sometimes promotions where you can redeem your points for gift cards with a 20-percent bonus. When these promotions are available, you will often see them inside the reward portals at big banks, such as Chase or American Express. In this example, you'd be about to get a twenty-four-dollar gift card for only 2,000 points (since the 20-percent bonus would be added on). For some people who would value gifting gift cards to people, this could be a fair route, but you would have to look out for promotions when they are presented.

Through a portal, you can purchase airline tickets and book hotels and rental cars for a premium rate on your points when compared to the average rate at a merchant site, but only if you have the top travel cards, such as the Chase Sapphire Preferred, Chase Sapphire Reserve, or the American Express Platinum cards.

Each of the Chase cards I referenced will offer a bonus on points when redeeming them through the Chase Ultimate Rewards travel portal. The Sapphire Preferred will give you a 25-percent bonus, whereas the Sapphire Reserve will give you a 50-percent bonus. In the example of the Sapphire Reserve, a 50-percent bonus on 100,000 points would give you the redemption value of 150,000 points! This essentially increases the value of points in this example from $1,000 to $1,500! This is one of the many reasons I always recommend the Chase Sapphire Reserve to people who have any intention of traveling. The benefits on this card alone have saved me tens of thousands of dollars through the free travel it has provided to me. Another thing that is exceptionally cool about this card, and the 50-percent bonus, is that you can combine your points from other Chase cards over to the Chase Sapphire Reserve. If you are someone that has (or plans to have) a variety of Chase cards for your personal and business life, you can use the card accordingly to accumulate the points effectively, and then before redeeming them, combine them with the Reserve so you can take advantage of the epic 50-percent bonus. Aside from the Sapphire Preferred, Ink Preferred, and Sapphire Reserve, all points are only redeemable at a 1:1 ratio. With that said, to get the most value from your Chase points, if you plan to redeem them for travel using the Chase Ultimate Rewards portal, it is best to have the Chase Sapphire Reserve so you can take advantage of this generous bonus.

Additionally on the Chase Sapphire Reserve, they also have a feature called "Pay-Yourself-Back," which allows you to give yourself a statement credit for select travel and dining purchases while taking advantage of the 50-percent bonus. This is a very unique feature that not many people know about! This essentially gives you a 30-percent discount on the purchases you choose to pay yourself back on via points. For example, if you have a $1,500 dining expense on your Chase Sapphire Reserve, you could use 100,000 points to issue you a $1,500 credit to your statement to cover this expense. The 50-percent bonus on points just gave you a 30-percent discount on that dining expense! Not bad! I have personally done this, and it was incredibly helpful with cash flow during that specific month.

Before moving to strategies on how to get higher than a 50-percent bonus on points, I want to dive into one of the features that American Express offers that also allows you receive a 30-percent discount on select travel expenses. To take advantage of this, you first would need to have the American Express Platinum or American Express Business Platinum. Secondly, this will only work when you book flights on your "selected airline." At American Express each year, you have the option to choose a "selected airline" to spend a $200 airline credit toward for incidentals but also to take advantage of a 30-percent rebate on points for this specific airline. You will also receive the 30-percent rebate on points on any business or first-class ticket, but I use credit to pay for those, so I generally don't get value from that specifically. But, if you have United Airlines chosen as your selected airlines for the year, you'd receive a 30-percent rebate on points anytime you are redeeming American Express points for United Airlines flights. However, it's crucial you have the airline selected before you make the booking to receive the rebate, so I would highly recommend doing this first. You can only pick a selected airline once per year, so pick wisely. When I booked a flight for my girlfriend and I to fly to Egypt, the total cost for two round-trip United Airlines tickets was 150,000 points, or $1,500. Since I booked the flights with American Express points from my Business Platinum card and had my selected airline as United Airlines, I received a rebate of 50,000 points. This alone essentially saved me $500! This was one of the most memorable trips of my life too. The reason we went was to skydive over the Pyramids of Giza, which I'll actually include a photo below, a very surreal moment that was partially enabled by leveraging my credit card points.

While we are on the topic of American Express, there is an additional strategy that allows you to get a 25-percent bonus on your points. This is a very unique one and only possible through the American Express Platinum (not even the American Express Business Platinum). As of 2019, American Express came out with a co-branded Platinum card with Charles Schwab, which allowed its holder to transfer American Express points from the portal into your Charles Schwab investment account with a 25-percent bonus. The bonus isn't crazy high, but if you were in a position where you needed cash much more than points, this would definitely be the best route to cash out your American Express points. The only two requirements would be having the American Express Platinum card and having a Charles Schwab account under your name you could transfer the points into.

These options will give you a pretty good return for your points, but we can do even better.

This part brings up a topic that I want to really emphasize the power of. Transfer partners are your best friends in this section on travel for credit points redemption. You are going to find deals that blow standard redemption strategies out of the water. The optimal way to use your credit card points is to find transfer partner deals and move your points from one location to another before redeeming. Some airlines are travel partners with certain credit card companies and will enable you to get a very nice multiple on your points. This process takes just a little bit more research and strategy than just opening an online travel agency and searching for your flight, but I promise you, it's well worth it. I've planned entire vacations on nothing but points and using this method, and once you get the hang of it, you'll be able to as well.

The strategy starts with understanding where you have points and where you have the option of transferring them to, based on the reward program transfer partners. Next, you will want to start researching flight and hotel deals through your reward programs, such as Chase and American Express. While doing your research, you will want to start noting down what airlines and hotels have the best options for your stay. For example, if Delta has ideal direct flights for you from Atlanta, Georgia, to your desired destination, we will want to compare the number of points that it will cost on Chase and American Express to the number of points that Delta will charge you if you were to book directly on Delta.com. To view the flights in the number of points it would cost you, you must first have a Delta SkyMiles account. After you have a Delta SkyMiles account created (in this example), you will want to search for the same good flights on Delta SkyMiles that you're seeing on American Express. More often than not, you will see the number of points the airline will charge you directly will be less than what reward programs like Chase or American Express will offer. Once you can verify that the deal is much better with the airline directly, you have the ability to transfer points into Delta SkyMiles. For example, if you are seeing the same flight offered for 80,000 on American Express but only 40,000 on Delta, it's a no brainer. However, the receiving rewards program must be a "transfer partner" of the program you are sending points from. If you had American Express points you could transfer, you will want to run a search to see if Delta SkyMiles is a transfer partner of American Express. I will list the transfer partner of both Chase Ultimate Rewards and American Express Membership Rewards below, so let's see if Delta makes it on the list.

Chase Ultimate Reward Transfer Partners:

- Aer Lingus AerClub
- Air Canada Aeroplan
- Air France-KLM Flying Blue
- British Airways Executive Club
- Emirates Skywards
- Iberia Plus
- JetBlue TrueBlue
- Singapore Airlines KrisFlyer
- Southwest Airlines Rapid Rewards
- United MileagePlus
- Virgin Atlantic Flying Club
- IHG Rewards Club
- Marriott Bonvoy
- World of Hyatt

American Express Membership Reward Partners

- Asia Miles
- British Airways
- Delta Skymiles
- Emirates Skywards
- Etihad Guest
- Finnair
- Flying Blue (Air France / KLM)
- Iberia Plus
- Marriott Bonvoy

- Qantas Frequent Flyer
- Scandinavian Airlines
- Singapore Airlines KrisFlyer
- Virgin Atlantic Flying Club

And boom! We both see Delta Skymiles on the list. That means you will be able to send points from American Express to Delta SkyMiles. I attached a screenshot from the American Express portal that shows you the transfer value you would receive. Most airlines transfer at 1:1 but will also sometimes offer a promotion that gives you a higher multiple. To transfer the points, you would click the "transfer points" tab inside the American Express travel portal, click the desired airline, choose the amount you'd like to transfer, enter your airline account number, and submit it. Transfers are generally instant. Two notes I want to emphasize is that once points are transferred out of Chase or American Express, they cannot be transferred back. It's important you're desired flight is bookable, and you can book it soon after you transfer the point over and ensure you are able to lock it in. Secondly, I'm generally not one to speculate in terms of transferring points to an airline for a booking in the future. I am only transferring the points if I plan to immediately make the reservation. Sometimes, as seen in the screenshot below, there will be promotions, such as with AeroMexico in this example, which gives you a higher multiple. In this scenario, it could make sense to transfer them into AeroMexico if you are confident you will end up using the point at some point relatively soon. Really, I would only transfer them in for a future reservation if the promotion is extra incentivizing and I am positive that I will be able to utilize them. In the scenario you transfer them in and end up not using them, it would be sort of a waste.

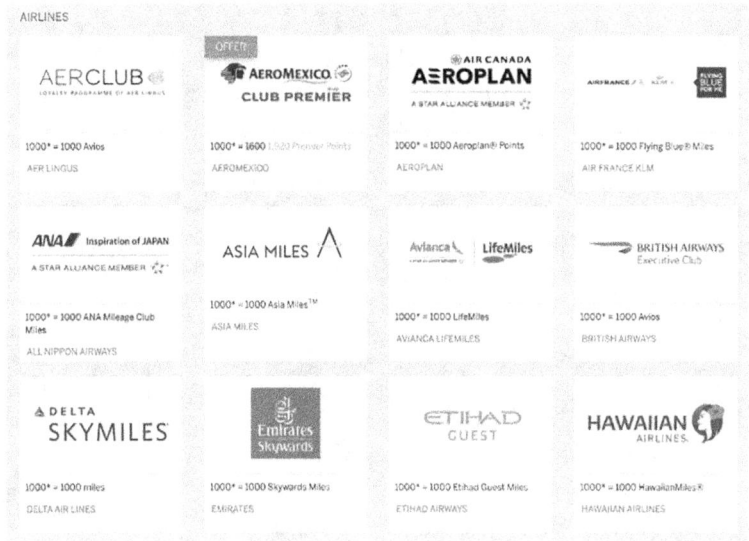

In terms of how to get the absolute best value through this strategy, you will want to use it on long-haul flights or ones that have a high face value. You can certainly save on domestic flights, but you will certainly find a better multiple on your savings for international flights, domestic flights over four hours, or any first-class ticket. The higher the face value of the seat, the more room for savings. If you are short on time, I wouldn't bother with this strategy on short domestic flights, but on the other type of ticket I mentioned, I certainly would if you'd like to maximize the value on your points. Personally, this strategy has saved me hundreds of thousands of points. When I booked flights from Los Angeles to Athens, Greece, I was able to book two business class tickets for only 164,000 points + $500 (total value of $2,140). The face value on these seats was well over $10K, so I was able to score almost a 5X multiple! Here is a screenshot of the points it cost me and a photo of me asleep on the direct flight to Greece:

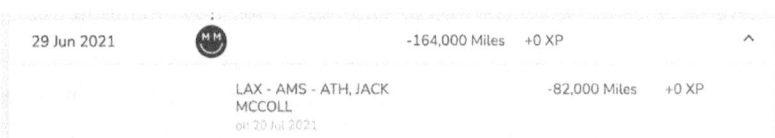

To really emphasize my point here, let me show you another example of a search that I literally just ran before writing this. In the below screenshots, you will see a business class seat from Los Angeles to Athens, Greece, on January 25, 2022. In the first screenshot, you will be able to see that it's available to book for $7,474. However, in the following screenshot, you will be able to see that it would only cost me 55,000 points + $251. Since each point is valued at 1 cent, the points would be valued at $550, and after adding the $251 fee, that would cost me a total of $771. Wow, I am actually blown away writing this out, we just found a 10X multiple on our points! That's the true power of transfer partners right there!

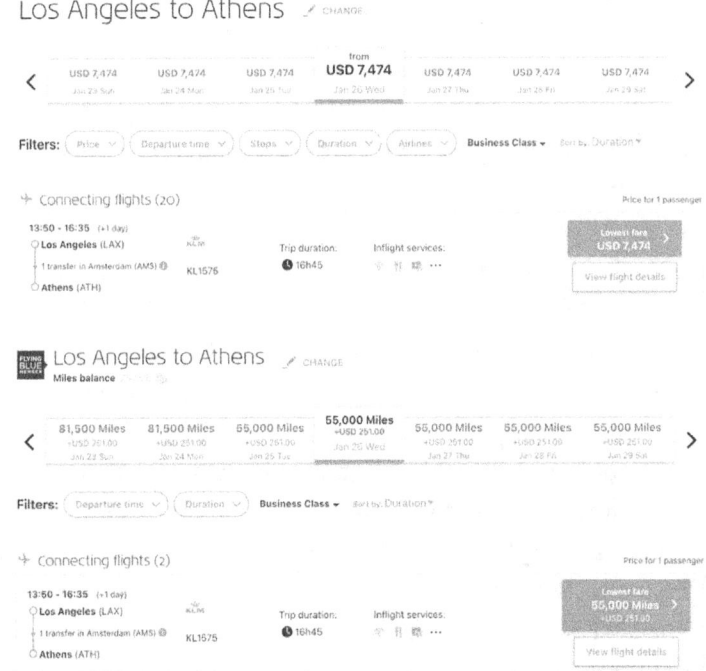

In conclusion of how we did this, let me lay out the steps for you so it's nice and clear:

1. Search for flights on either Chase Ultimate Rewards or American Express Membership Rewards portal;
2. Locate your most ideal routes;
3. Create an account with the airline that offers those routes, and choose "pay with points" while running a search for the same flight on their portal;

4. Verify which airline will give you the best multiple on your points;
5. Figure out if either Chase or American Express is a transfer partner to their rewards program;
6. Transfer points from Chase or American Express to the desired transfer partner;
7. Book your flight with the points; and
8. Enjoy your free trip at an epic multiple of your points!

It is as simple as that! Just a couple of extra steps can save you thousands of dollars.

The select airlines that were listed work best for Amex and Chase users, but it doesn't just stop there. You'll find hotels that work with these kinds of programs, multiple card companies too. When it comes to hotels, the deals can get even crazier, it's just a matter of knowing what properties offer the best deals and the best time frames in the year to book your trip for, which can save hours of tedious research. As with many of these steps, there are some more steps than the standard searching for and booking a flight or trip. If you feel that you can do it effectively with this book, then go ahead and try it out and find the best deals for your travel goals. But if you feel that you need a hand through some of the steps, this section is entirely covered through a variety of screenshare step-by-step examples in the Credit Stacking mentorship program, along with the rest of the credit point redemption strategies we've been covering. Ultimately, I just want these strategies to work for you. While running a business, you're going to find that expenses related to your business rack up very quickly. These cards you're using to purchase inventory, subscriptions, or shipping expenses can accumulate these points much faster than the standard consumer will. When it comes to certain transfer partners, I have a list of the best partners who offer the best value for points based on the rewards program they are coming from, which can reduce the amount of research someone has to put in when booking their trips. The partners who offer the best multiple often change, so it's nice to have this information provided to you so the entrepreneurs in our group can focus on growing their business and investing. The key point of this process is using those accumulated points optimally and budgeting your point redemptions to fully cover your trips. This is not as hard as it may seem at first glance, and hopefully you're already getting a hang of the process.

For the most simple way to use points, you can always just redeem your points for a statement credit. This may help if you aren't able to use travel points or simply have different needs for the current stage in your life. Maybe you have a year that is keeping you glued to your projects, and you won't be able to use the points but would love to maximize profits by paying off some credit card balances using points. You can do this, and it's totally fine. There's no rule saying you have to use these points on travel miles. But when it comes to optimizing returns, sometimes the ideal option is to save up on your miles for a couple of years and then use them to help you go on that trip you've needed to get your mind off things. Maybe it can help you focus better too. If you remember, we did discuss that when pursuing a more efficient environment to work from, you are best off if you separate yourself from distractions. Like I said then, I've gone and gotten hotel rooms to just separate myself from the things to do at home. If you need to use some points on a room or trip where you can optimize your work performance, then use it and get that grind on!

These points are supposed to work for you, not you working for your points. If there are any methods in this book that don't return the needs you had them for or don't make your life easier and your goals more attainable, then do not use them for that purpose. Don't feel you have to use them for any one usage. These tips are simply here to enable effective usage of these points in an optimal fashion.

GAINING STATUS WITH HOTELS

Now that you've gotten down to a way to redeem points for miles through transfer partners, let's talk hotel status. Just like there is a way to maximize the value you are getting on your credit card points, there are ways to maximize the enjoyment you are getting out of your hotel stays, and we do this through achieving hotel status. We're talking about room upgrades, free breakfast, late check out, and many other benefits that will enhance your hotel experience. This section isn't too complicated, especially if you've already gone through the section about flight points.

There are a few ways to get status, some you can achieve through credit, and others without credit at all. If you go through the credit route, it's much faster and can provide more benefits to you, so let's start there. When you are researching what travel credit card to get, you will want to consider the benefits that come with each card. If you plan to stay in hotels in the near future, one thing to look at is what hotel you will get at least Gold status at. Before I dive into the way to get high status and the cards that offer them, let me list the status benefits below for Gold status.

- **Hilton Honor Gold**
    - Room upgrades
    - Complimentary breakfast
    - 5th consecutive award night free
    - Late check out
    - Free internet
    - 80% bonus points on hotel stays
- **Marriott Bonvoy Gold Status**
    - Room upgrades
    - 5th consecutive reward night free
    - Late check out
    - Free internet

- 25% bonus points on hotel stays
- Welcome amenity points

There are a variety of credit cards that will secure you with Marriott Bonvoy Gold or Hilton Honor Gold, but there is only one credit card that will give you Gold status to both. When it comes to offering hotel status, the American Express Platinum and American Express Business Platinum are the leader in the market. By getting approved for this card, you will be eligible to activate your Gold status at each hotel brand so you can start taking advantage of the great benefits. However, to activate the Gold status, you have to "enroll" through the American Express Membership Rewards portal. It's very quick to do but crucial to do beforehand if you'd like to enjoy the benefits. I can tell you from personal experience that room upgrades, late check out, and a welcome gift make the experience quite nice! If you travel a lot or plan to for business or pleasure, you may be missing out by not taking advantage of these perks. If one of the American Express Platinum cards isn't a top choice for you, there are a variety of other travel cards that can help you achieve this status, which I'll list below:

- Hilton Honors American Express Surpass–Hilton Gold Status, with spend minimum for Diamond
- Marriott Bonvoy Brilliant American Express–Marriott Gold Elite
- IHG Rewards Club Premier Credit Card–IHG Platinum Elite

Here is what the cards look like so you can easily recognize them.

If you are someone who travels or plans to travel, I would highly suggest adding a hotel credit card to your stack. They normally also include things, such as statement credit, which you can use at the hotel and give you up to 7–17X points per dollar spent. Getting the multiple on points while spending is huge, so I hope you can take advantage of it.

TRAVEL BENEFITS WITH CREDIT (AND TOP CARDS)

For many people, the process of traveling to a destination can be an exhausting or uncomfortable experience. Often, airports can be hectic and uncomfortable. But just like everything I have outlined in this book, there is always a way to flip the average script to create an incredible experience out of it. When I was traveling in my early twenties, I traveled like an average person since I only had access to average information. I waited in lines, I wasn't prioritized, I sat in economy class, I had to pay for my checked bags, and had to pay for my food in the airports. But over the last few years, I've been able to find ways to enhance most parts of the traveling process. Airports were always an experience that I didn't necessarily look forward to, but now, with the strategies I'm about to outline, I actually look forward to my time spent in airports.

Through the same way we were able to gain free benefits through credit cards to accumulate and redeem points, we are able to unlock incredible benefits that can enhance many parts of our travel experience. I learned that a variety of top credit cards give you access to airport lounges, which offer comfy chairs to lounge in, premier Wi-Fi (which I can actually work effectively), complimentary food and drinks, private rooms, and sometimes even showers. When I learned about airport lounges and how to get access to them, it all clicked for me on how the upper class travel. With the knowledge and access to airport lounges, why would anyone ever hang out in the general area with uncomfortable chairs, Medicare Wi-Fi, and minimal privacy? It didn't make sense to me at first why most people didn't take advantage of this secret, but then I remember, like most secrets, it's all just a matter of education and understanding how to apply it to your life. The education is knowing what credit cards offer airport lounge access and knowing the process of personal credit optimization that is necessary to actually get approved for these top credit cards. Most cards that offer airport lounge access are the top cards at its respective bank, so not every average person off the street is able to get approved for them. But fortunately for you after reading this book, you should now have a good understanding of how to get approved these top cards.

Now that I have access to a variety of airport lounges, I will intentionally arrive at the airport early, not only to ensure I make my flights, but also because it's comfortable, and I enjoy it. I'll roll in with my membership, grab some free food, set up my laptop at a nice desk, hop on the premier Wi-Fi, and work until I need to board my flight. This is another major way I am able to get so much work done while I travel. Some of these lounges are incredibly nice, which allows me to get great work done before boarding my flight.

When we look at each of the cards that I outline below, you will see each card can give you access to a different lounge or different group of lounges. Some cards give you access to just one lounge, but others will give you access to lounges all around the world.

Top credit cards that give you airport lounge access:

- The Platinum Card from American Express
    - Access to 1,000+ lounges worldwide
    - Access to the American Express Centurion Lounge
    - Access to Delta Sky Club Lounge when flying Delta
- The Business Platinum Card from American Express
    - Business card that gives you access to 1,000+ lounges
    - Access to 1,000+ lounges
    - Access to the American Express Centurion Lounge
    - Access to Delta Sky Club Lounge when flying Delta
- Chase Sapphire Reserve
    - Access to 1,000+ lounges worldwide
    - Gives you large credits at a variety of airport restaurants
- Capital One Venture X
    - Access to 1,000+ lounges worldwide
    - Access to Capital One Lounges
- Citi© / AAdvantage Executive World Elite Mastercard©
    - Access to American Airlines Admiral Lounges
- Delta SkyMiles Reserve American Express Card
    - Access to Delta Sky Club Lounges
- Delta SkyMiles Reserve Business American Express Card
    - Access to Delta Sky Club Lounges
- United Club Infinite Card
    - Access to United Club Lounges

As you can see, there are quite a few travel cards that can give you access to airport lounges. If you are an avid traveler and don't already have airport lounge access, I would highly consider incorporating one of these travel cards in your plan to acquire more credit. If it came down to one travel card from that list that is most effective for lounge access, I would pick one of the American Express Platinum cards. However, it does come with a steep annual fee, which is something to consider. I personally have the American Express Business Platinum, Chase Sapphire Reserve, and Chase United Club card. The Chase

Sapphire Reserve doesn't give you access to the Centurion Lounges or Delta Sky Club Lounges, but it does give me access to over 1,000 airport lounges worldwide and credits at a variety of airport restaurants. If I was a little more price aware of the annual fee, and also to factor other benefits between the two cards, I would pick the Chase Sapphire Reserve. This card has saved me tens of thousands of dollars through its benefits and point accumulation/redemption and is my favorite personal credit card on the market.

These cards can help secure this time for you to work or relax and never have to bother with a stressful airport experience again. Say goodbye to smelly seats covered in crumbs and having no privacy when you are waiting for your flight. By utilizing the cards we've discussed, you'll guarantee a better travel experience through the airport when you travel.

GLOBAL ENTRY & TSA PRE-CHECK

That tackles the issues with layovers and stressful, crowded airports. But what about checking in and security? There are two simple methods to deal with that part.

1. Global Entry
2. TSA Pre-Check
3. CLEAR

These two methods can be used with each other to deliver stress-free access through security. With global entry, you can skip the customs line when checking back into the US. This usually costs around one hundred dollars but can be accessed for free through a variety of top travel cards. The same can be said for TSA Pre-Check, which usually costs eighty-five dollars, that allows you the ability to move ahead in line at the airport without removing your shoes waiting in a long security line. To take airport security on outbound flights to the next level, CLEAR allows you to even skip the TSA Pre-Check line.

If you are an avid international traveler, then Global Entry is a must. What this does is allows you to essentially skip the immigration line. With Global Entry, I have personally never waited in line to get back into the United States. Without, you'll most likely be waiting thirty to ninety minutes in the immigration line. If you don't have Global Entry, then you might have already experienced this. After a long international flight, the last thing you will want to be doing is standing in a long line, so the time saving and convenience really comes into play and makes your return to the United States much more enjoyable.

TSA Pre-Check, as you may have seen, allows you to wait in a separate line than the GA line. This allows you to not only keep your shoes on but also can save you thirty+ minutes of waiting. Even for keeping your shoes on ability, this is a no brainer. Bending over to untie my shoes and walk on the dirty floor through the scanner just to have to bend over and retie them is not a great time. TSA Pre-Check only takes a short interview so they can collect some basic information and fingerprint you. After that, it's valid for five years. Again, absolute no brainer, especially when you can get it for free through credit cards. Most top travel cards offer this as a statement credit when you use the card to pay for it.

With CLEAR, I literally haven't waited in an airport line in over a year; it's incredible. The only exception here is when the airport doesn't have CLEAR. Not all of them do, but most of the large airports in the United States do. In the scenario, an average person has to wait thirty to forty-five minutes in the GA line on a busy airport morning; you would be rolling through airport security within five minutes tops. It's incredibly easy to enroll. First, you will have to pay the $179 with the credit card, which offer the statement credit (such as the American Express Platinum), arrive at a CLEAR kiosk at the airport, let the machine scan your eye for biometric data, provide other basic personal info, and boom, now you are a CLEAR member. Here is how the process works when you arrive at the airport when you have CLEAR. All you need to do is roll up to the kiosk, let the machine scan your eyes, and show them your boarding pass where you are then escorted to the very front of the line, where a CLEAR employee will confirm with the TSA employee that your identity has been verified, and you're off to the security belt. No lines, ever!

A key hack to specify is to sign up for Global Entry first. Since the selected credit cards will give you either a statement credit for Global Entry or TSA Pre-Check, you will want to choose to purchase Global Entry since it comes with TSA Pre-Check but not the other way around. This will simply put you in the best position for both leaving and coming back to the US. Not having to go through long lines and walk around in your socks before you run to your gate and are stuck in a crowded boarding area for hours will put your travel back in your control and give you the chance to focus on why you were traveling to begin with.

The options in this chapter are limitless and almost impossible to fit in a single chapter. I could go on and on with the benefits and travel hacks that come with credit, but I'll leave it there as those are the most important and impactful to enhance your travel experience. I always like to steer you toward my program I've developed online, Credit Stacking, because I do an in-depth explanation for the perks and strategies that we've gone over to ensure you are taking full advantage of the benefits that are available to you. This part of the Credit Stacking process is one that I am incredibly passionate about and wanted to share with you with the hopes that you could use it to go to more places in less time, not having to stop whenever life gets busy. You can travel on points, work from an airport lounge, and do your conference calls from a relaxing hotel room with a pool and fitness center five steps away from you. The coaching calls we do on a weekly basis in Credit Stacking are great because I will walk our members through any new travel hacks that arise and break them down step by step so others can benefit. For example, on the recent coaching call, I outlined my exact strategy, which allowed me to use American Express points to book a five-night stay at the Ritz-Carlton in the Maldives. If I would have paid cash for this, it would have cost me almost $11,000. However, through my strategy, I was able to book it for only 280,000 points, which, at a 1:1 point ratio, comes out to a cost of $2,800. The only expense associated with the hotel reservation is $700 per person to get to the island from the main island. I was able to gain those points through sign-up bonuses and organic spending, so it was essentially free for me to book this. All I needed was the education that I went over in the book to make it happen. I Might as well show you if you don't think I'm making it up. Check out the screenshots below, where you can see the cash total of $10,797 in the first screenshot compared to the 280,000 points I used on the reservation.

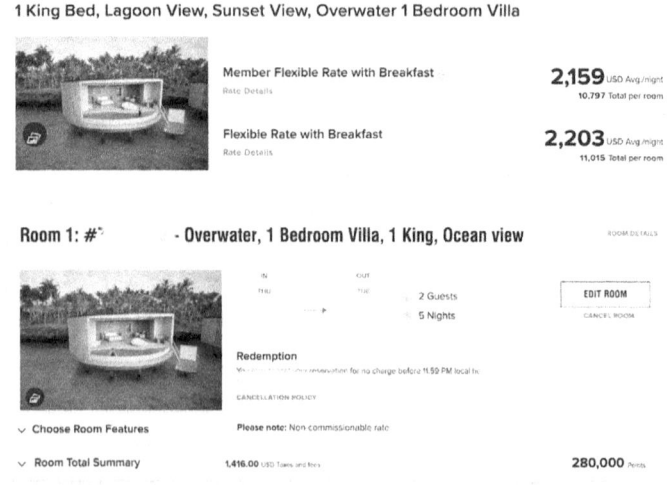

This is the best as it gets for maximizing Marriott points. In this example I'm getting a 4X multiple on value. You can do this all around the world too. I'm also going to use this same strategy on my trip to the St. Regis in Bora Bora this year. When you know these strategies, the entire world opens up to you. If you are reading this book, you are not here to live an average life. It's time to turn up the heat and full send the next few years with the information you are learning. When you use these strategies, feel free to tag me on IG or shoot me a DM (@kingofdebt). I'd be happy to see you using them!

What's cool about creating an online community:

In the course, as well as the community that you'll meet on our social media, at the Credit Stacking page on Facebook, are chances to network and learn about deals and plans that can secure relaxing and stress-free travel for you. Here you can be living your best life and utilizing your hard-earned revenue to buy you opportunities to see the world and experience things that you never thought you'd be able to experience. Unlike some of the other chapters, this chapter is primarily driven by your network if you're looking for optimal returns on travel points.

Your network will end up always being your most valuable asset. The author and entrepreneur Seth Godin once said that "Networking that matters is helping people achieve their goals," and I could not agree more. This community that you're beginning to form around you in your entrepreneurship life is one that will last and help you and others achieve your goals. The tips in this book and the strategies you read here and will find that I have a long, extensive list of great cards that give you so many options for so many benefits on the course too, with links and specific instructions for each one that give you the best chances for approval and using them for optimal results. Keep the same discipline here that you've already utilized to raise your business capital, and these tips and tricks you've just learned can transform your work-life harmony in a way you never thought was possible.

CHAPTER 7
THE ROAD TO INDEPENDENCE

You've made it. You've learned secrets to business credit that many people don't even know exist. If you're keeping accountable with your journaling I mentioned in chapter 1, this is worth a dedicated page to commemorate. From here is where the real journey starts. After I initially learned the information I've shared here, my entire life changed. I was shocked at how much further I could have been in my goals had I known these techniques a few years earlier. Those times that people like you and I spent raising capital through slower or riskier methods like our own personal savings, friends and family, or high-interest business loans may feel like a waste of time. And you might feel like looking at them as time spent with no return. However, if you write anything down from this book, make sure it's this: You learned something in those times. You learned and grew as an individual. Even if the only thing you learned is that those methods are not for you, then that was a lesson learned through experience, the kind most likely to stick with you. The next steps are crucial for you. While raising your capital and applying the principles I've shared with you, you will be on the path to independence as a business, entrepreneur, and individual. There's a quote by Grant Cardone that has stuck with me in times like the exponential growth you'll experience through credit stacking.

He said that "Independence is something you have to work hard to get and harder to keep."

The independence you'll experience using these tools will grow you into an individual that you would not have recognized several years ago, but you can't plateau. You can't make that your norm. You've got to push past the plateau and toward the next steep climb. Get yourself to that place of freedom where you can enjoy your life, where you're spending your life, who you're spending it with, and how you're able to spend it. That is how I try to live; spending every day waking up and thinking about what I can do today that will help me achieve. You will gain the independence you desire if you push on through the many plateaus you'll face along the way.

Once you get to that place where you know you're seeing more and more of your goals reached, make sure you stop and pay it forward. This is really the last thing I want to leave you with. Pay it forward to help those who are on the same journey as you. I didn't write this book or lay out my online course as someone who is retired and already at the end of my journey. The truth is I am right there with you all. I am still a work in progress, finding my success each new day. And when you stop along the way to help your fellow entrepreneurs and success-driven collaborators, you will find that you, too, will still wake up every new day, ready to make each day your achievement and to grind out those goals. Most definitely give yourself the time and period of growth necessary to boost your success to a point where supporting the dreams of others doesn't come at the price of your own. You'll find that you can do it all for yourself and feel great. But when you turn around and give back pieces of what you've found along the way, you'll feel a sense of fulfillment that your own personal success cannot compensate for.

Get your grind going and keep disciplined.

Get access to as much low-interest capital as you can.

Build your dream life through meeting your goals and your milestones daily.

Then, one day, when you can look back and see the results speaking for themselves, turn around and give somebody a few steps back behind you a hand. Give your ideas and results over to the next generation of dreamers behind you and help them achieve the things you have come to enjoy.

I hope that I have been able to help mentor you here and that you've come away with the confidence you will need to achieve your goals and attain the dreams you have set in front of you. I wish you the best in your grind and the absolute maximum results from your credit.

You've learned several very important principles and gained several tools in this book. While I want you to be able to use these tools here in your life and pursuit of success, I understand it won't always be easy. There will be obstacles at every turn, distractions throughout your day, and the desire to quit may sometimes catch you off-guard. I am confident that you'll overcome and learn from these opportunities. At the same time, I know that having a coach is always helpful when pursuing a successful life. Without my mentors, I'd never have learned any of the techniques and mindsets that I've discussed with you. If you want to know more about Credit Stacking and join a community of hundreds of like-minded individuals, please consider joining our group. I'll add some information at the end of this book to help you get signed up. Through this program, you can find resources like a template for credit analysis, step-by-step instructions for credit card applications with links and instructions, access to all our internal database resources that will save time and mistakes, receive personal introductions to my business relationship managers, and so much more. There's also the opportunity to join our community on Facebook for discussions, instructions, networking, and one-on-one mentoring. This chance to network with other high-performance entrepreneurs is one that you will not find in many other places. Each of them is not only working on a similar plan as you but is also working through the same coursework and techniques as you will be doing. What better way to grow and learn the material better than to discuss it and network with others? While I've made sure to add as much information as I can in this book to help you, there really is no substitute for the final service that I offer in the Credit Stacking program. I will personally work with you on coaching calls and walk you through your questions, concerns, or plans that you might have for your funding. I've told you before that my success has largely been due to the mentors and networks that I have surrounded myself with. This is something I believe deeply. You can try and go it alone, and you very well might make it far. But I can promise you it will inhibit your growth in the same way raising capital without credit will inhibit your funding growth. It is my hope that this book will give you the knowledge you've needed to kick-start your dreams and that I can continue to help you out online.

Thank you for taking the time to read this book. I wish you the absolute best on your journey!

If you are interested to learn more, I encourage you to book a free strategy session with my team so we can lay out a personalized game plan for you; please head to Creditstacking.com.

I will also include links below where you can access pages to see my podcast features, online publications, and dozens of video testimonies that highlight Credit Stacking student success.

Podcast Features: CreditStacking.com/Podcasts

Online Publications (Bloomberg, Entrepreneur, USA Today, etc.): CreditStacking.com/Press

Credit Stacking Video Testimonies: CreditStacking.com/Success

I will also include some screenshots below that highlight some of the success that Credit Stacking students have seen.

$203,000 in approval business credit in three months

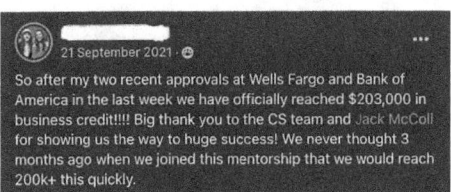

$182,000 in approved business credit

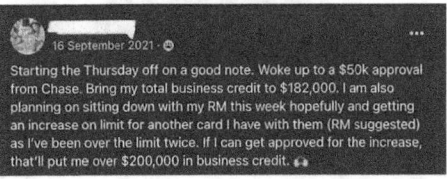

$170,000 in approved credit

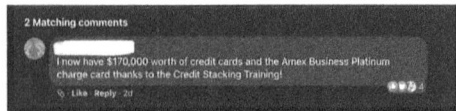

$135,000 in approved 0-percent interest business credit

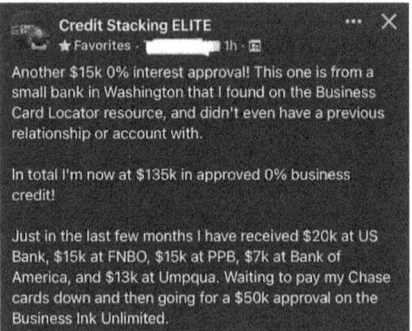

$69,000 of approved 0-percent interest business credit

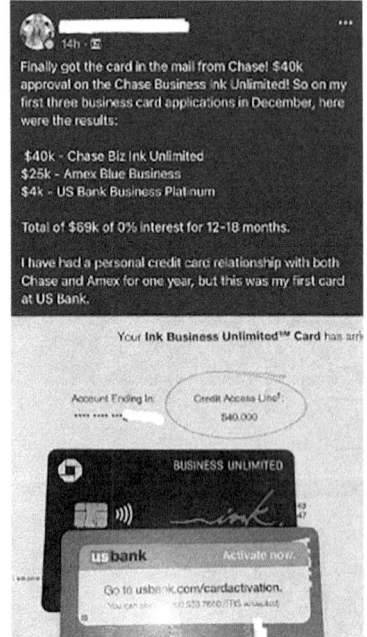

$75,000 0-percent interest Chase business credit card approval

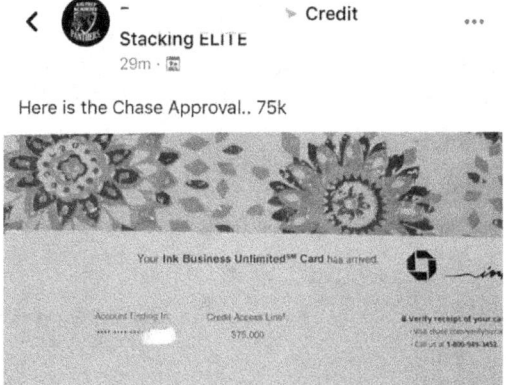

$70,000 0-percent interest Chase business credit card approval

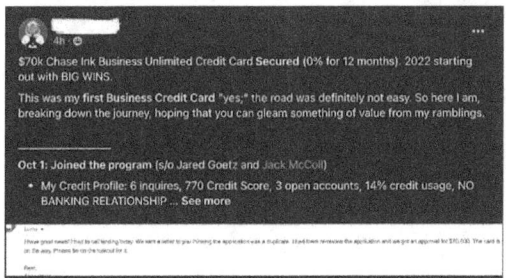

$50,000 0-percent interest Chase business credit card approval

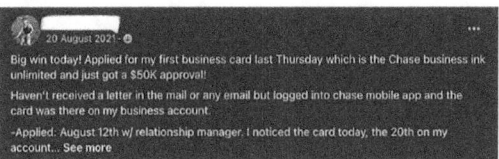

$50,000 0-percent interest Chase business credit card approval

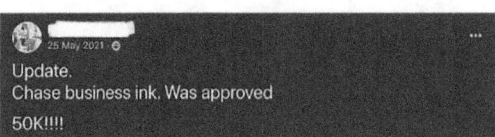

CREDIT STACKING

$50,000 0-percent interest Chase business credit card approval

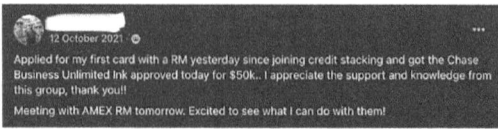

$50,000 0-percent interest Chase business credit card approval

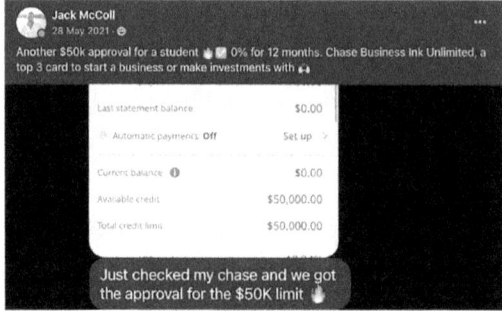

GLOSSARY

Credit Stacking Terms:

- Point accumulation
    - Refers to the points accumulated from the activity on your credit card that can be redeemed for various perks.
- Point redemption
    - Using the accumulated points for free benefits.
- Annual fee
    - Fee that you pay to use the credit card. Usually billed yearly.
- Balance transfer
    - Transfer of debt from one card account to another.
- Credit repair
    - The process of disputing anything on your credit history within a certain period to fix issues that may affect your credit score.
- Inquiry sweep
    - A removal of any hard inquiry that is not attached to any one account.
- Bankruptcy
    - Wiping the slate clean of all debt. This shows on your credit score for some time but can removed through credit repair.

- Spending power
    - Different from credit limit in that the more you spend on an unlimited card, the higher it can go.
- Credit limit
    - The limit of debt that you can use from any one card.
- Cash back
    - Money given back as an incentive to use a credit card.
- Savings account
    - Limited number of transactions per month.
- Checking account
    - Unlimited number of transactions per month.
- Foreign transaction fee
    - Fee that you are charged for using a card outside of a certain country.
- Debt-to-income ratio (DTI)
    - The amount of income you have versus the amount of outstanding debt you have.
- Grace period
    - The period after your statement closes until your bill is due.
- Interest rate
    - The rate that you will be charged for using debt.
- Intro annual percentage rate (APR)
    - An introductory period where a discounted, or in some cases, 0-percent interest rate is applied to your account to promote usage.
- Minimal monthly payment
    - The minimal amount that you need to pay on a card or other debt account to not be overdue for a payment.
- Prime rate
    - The rate of interest that you can qualify for with good credit.

Glossary

- Cash advance
    - Any time you liquidate money out of a credit card for use as cash. Usually at a very high interest rate.
- Line of credit
    - Certain amount of money that you are able to borrow at any given time from a lender.
- Soft inquiry
    - When a creditor looks at your credit without pulling your credit directly.
- Hard inquiry
    - Any time a lender looks directly at your credit.
- Billing cycle
    - Date interval that the statement is billed
- Capital
    - Money used as an asset.
- Cosigner
    - Someone who signs on with debt for you to pad risk in case you default. Typically required for someone with no credit history.
- Credit score
    - FICO or VantageScore. What the banks look at to determine the level of risk they take on if they approve you for credit.
- Creditor
    - Anyone loaning you money. In the case of credit stacking, it's typically a national bank with a credit card that they offer.
- Bureau
    - Organization that rates and stores credit scores.
- Sign-up bonus
    - Often in the form of a cash bonus if a certain amount is spent using the card in an introductory period.

- Roth IRA
    - A type of retirement account where you contribute your money up front free of tax to be taxed at a
- APY
    - The amount of interest billed on a credit balance if not paid off on time.
- OPM
    - "Other people's money." The concept of using the bank's money to fund your ventures, which is what this book is all about.
- EIN Number
    - The tax ID number that you will use when applying for business credit.
- LLC
    - Limited Liability Company. A popular way to structure a company where the individual is shielded from most forms of legal action or bankruptcy
- Charge Card
    - A card that does not have a preset limit. This is where the concept of spending power comes into play as the amount that you can use will increase the more that you use it.
- Secured Card
    - As a traditional credit card is called an unsecured credit card, it's pretty easy to understand the difference between the two. This type of card requires you to add money to the account before you can use it.
- Revolving credit
    - A credit agreement when a certain amount of debt is paid monthly on an amount of debt that resets after it is paid off.
- <30-day late payment
    - This kind of late payment is paid within thirty days from the due date but is not reported on your credit score.

Glossary

- \>30-day late payment
    - This kind of late payment is reported on your credit score and will hurt your chances of securing credit in the future.
- Charge off
    - When debt is so late in being paid that it is sold off to a debt collection agency.
- Manufacture Spend
    - Strategically spending on a card to get points or cash.
- Corporate credit
    - The next level up from consumer credit cards. This is reported differently from consumer credit through vendor tradelines.
- Transfer partners
    - Once points have been built up, you can transfer them to a transfer partner like a travel or hotel company, where you can redeem the points for travel miles or hotel rooms.
- 3X on dining
    - This is an example of a rate of points accumulated for a dining-related transaction.
- 50-percent bonus on redemption
    - Some travel portals will offer a bonus when you redeem your points through their portal.
- Bank relationship
    - Having history with a bank in the form of brokerage accounts, checking accounts, or any other account that may establish a history with that bank.
- Cash cleared
    - An availability of cash after a business account has been opened.
- Autopay
    - Simply automating your payments to ensure you don't miss minimum payments.

- Travel portal
    - Landing page to book travel transactions.
- Credit Line Increase
    - You can request an increase for your credit line after a certain amount of time or history with that bank.
- Vendor tradeline
    - When you can purchase a product for business purposes but then have to pay within a period of time. Typically, net 30, meaning payment is required within thirty days.

www.ingramcontent.com/pod-product-compliance
Lightning Source LLC
LaVergne TN
LVHW021821060526
838201LV00058B/3474